GARLIC

GARLIC

More than 65 recipes
celebrating garlic & wild garlic

Jenny Linford

photography by Clare Winfield

RYLAND PETERS & SMALL
LONDON • NEW YORK

Dedication
For my mother and father, with my love

Senior Designer Sonya Nathoo
Picture Manager Christina Borsi
Editors Gillian Haslam & Alice Sambrook
Head of Production Patricia Harrington
Creative Director Leslie Harrington
Editorial Director Julia Charles

Food Stylist Rachel Wood
Prop Stylist Jo Harris
Indexer Hilary Bird

First published in 2016 and reissued in 2019.
This revised edition published in 2025
by Ryland Peters & Small.
20–21 Jockey's Fields
London WC1R 4BW
and
1452 Davis Bugg Road
Warrenton, NC 27589

Text © Jenny Linford 2016, 2019, 2025
Design and commissioned photographs
© Ryland Peters & Small 2016, 2019, 2025
(see full photography credits on page 160)

ISBN: 978-1-78879-674-3

10 9 8 7 6 5 4 3 2 1

Printed and bound in China.

CIP data from the Library of Congress has been
applied for. A CIP record for this book is available
from the British Library.

Notes
• Both British (metric) and American (imperial
plus US cups) are included in these recipes; however,
it is important to work with one set of measurements
and not alternate between the two within a recipe.
• All eggs are medium (UK) or large (US), unless
specified as large, in which case US extra large should
be used. Uncooked or partially cooked eggs should
not be served to the very old, frail, young children,
pregnant women or those with compromised immune
systems.
• When a recipe calls for the grated zest of citrus fruit,
buy unwaxed fruit and wash well before using. If you
can only find treated fruit, scrub well
in warm soapy water before using.

MIX
Paper | Supporting
responsible forestry
FSC® C008047

Contents

Introduction

Garlic is audacious. Its pungent scent and powerful flavour – with each small clove packing a huge punch – have aroused strong feelings throughout history. This is an ingredient which, at times, has been scorned by the upper classes in society and frowned upon by a number of the world's religions. On the other hand, garlic's extraordinary ability to transform and invigorate dishes has made it a much-loved and essential flavouring in kitchens around the world. There is a distinctly democratic streak to its universal popularity; eaten with relish by the poor in many countries for many centuries, it has long been known to ancient civilizations, including those of China, India, Egypt, Greece and Rome.

The name 'garlic' originates from the Anglo Saxon word 'gar' meaning spear, a reference to the shape of the plant's leaves, though the plant itself is thought to be native to Central Asia. Otherwise known as *Allium sativum*, garlic's powerful flavour is released through crushing and chopping. One of the pleasures of cooking with it is learning how to adjust the level of 'garlic power' as required. For example, keeping a garlic clove whole makes it less powerful than cutting it into small pieces, in order to subtly infuse but not overwhelm a dish. A whole garlic clove fried in oil but then discarded, with the flavoured oil then used for cooking, is an effective method of adding its distinctive taste discreetly. A whole garlic clove placed in the cavity of a chicken before roasting has a similar effect, as has adding one to a slowly simmered casserole or sauce. Rubbing a salad bowl with a peeled garlic clove is a classic and elegant way of adding garlic notes.

When asked to write this book, I was thrilled. I had realized some years ago that all my favourite dishes contained garlic, so my affection for this extraordinary flavouring is deep and long-held. There are so many different ways of using garlic that, when it came to inspiration, I was spoilt for choice. French, Italian, Lebanese, Indian, Portuguese, Chinese, Thai – there are very few cuisines in the world in which garlic does not play a part. It is a truly cosmopolitan ingredient that features in many of the world's classic dishes, from Italy's homely pasta carbonara or Egypt's rustic ful medames to luxurious French coq au vin and Thailand's aromatic green curry. In writing this book, I've also embraced garlic-flavoured ingredients, such as wild garlic/ramps and garlic chives, on the grounds that they, too, deserve a place in a celebration of garlic.

Affordable and readily available, garlic is an everyday, almost humble ingredient, yet, when one stops to think about it, a remarkable one. If I had to choose one desert island ingredient, it would be garlic.

The many forms of garlic

Garlic

Known botanically as *Allium sativum*, there are two main subspecies of garlic (hardneck and softneck) and many further varieties, with greengrocers, delicatessens and farmers' markets all useful sources for purchasing. Garlic's powerful flavour is released when the cloves are broken, producing sulphur-containing compounds within the plant's cell walls. Garlic is usually sold in bulbs or heads, each containing separate cloves wrapped in a papery skin.

Wet garlic

Most garlic sold has been dried to preserve it. Wet garlic (or green garlic) is freshly harvested and sold as a new-season specialty. These young bulbs have not yet formed skins or split into cloves, so the whole head and stalk can be eaten. The flesh is moist and white with a mild flavour.

Elephant garlic

Striking in appearance, *Allium ampeloprasum* var. *ampeloprasum* is botanically classified as a leek rather than a garlic, although it possesses a mild garlic flavour. The large bulb contains large cloves, which can be used whole in dishes to good visual effect.

Black garlic

Originally from Korea, black garlic is a form of preserved garlic, created by gently heating heads of garlic for a long period of time. During this process, the cloves blacken in colour and the garlic changes texture, becoming soft. The flavour also mellows, losing the pungency of garlic, taking on instead smoky and balsamic vinegar notes. In cooking, black garlic is used for its flavour and its striking black appearance.

A selection of garlic bulbs, in their many glorious forms.

Smoked garlic

Garlic is smoked to transform its flavour, rather than to preserve it, giving a subtle smokiness to the cloves – while muting their natural pungency – and adding a dark brown hue to the papery wrapping.

Deep-fried garlic

Available ready-made in stores/supermarkets, this is produced by deep-frying finely minced garlic in oil until golden brown and crispy. A popular ingredient in Thai cuisine, deep-fried garlic is used to add crunchy texture and garlic flavour to a wide range of dishes.

Pickled garlic

Peeled garlic cloves are preserved in brine and vinegar, these have a crunchy texture and retain a strong garlic flavour, as well as a salty tanginess.

Garlic salt

A seasoning made by mixing salt with ground dried garlic, this has a distinctive garlic flavour and is a store cupboard substitute for fresh garlic.

Garlic scapes

Garlic scapes are flower stalks produced by hardneck garlic. They are harvested in late spring and prized as a seasonal delicacy. Bright green in appearance, they have a pleasant juicy texture and a sweet garlicky flavour. They can be used as a herb or a vegetable.

Wild garlic/ramps

Also known as ramsons, wood garlic or bear garlic, the plant *Allium ursinum* grows wild in shady woodlands in Europe, with its edible long green leaves possessing a definite garlic aroma and a subtle garlic flavour. In North America, wild garlic is 'ramps' or *Allium trioccum,* a very similar plant to *Allium ursinum.*

Garlic chives

Allium tuberosum, also known as Chinese chives, have long, flat, narrow, green leaves and a distinctive garlic flavour. In Chinese and Korean cookery they are used as flavouring and as a vegetable in stir-fries.

Mellow garlic

Garlic preparation and storage

When it comes to cooking with garlic, part of its versatility as a flavouring is that you can adjust the strength as required. Breaking down the garlic cells as you chop or crush a clove causes an enzyme reaction creating the compound which gives garlic its distinctive smell and flavour. So, when just a discreet garlic touch is required, adding a whole clove, unpeeled or peeled, to a dish such as a ragu works well. For gloriously powerful garlic, however, crushed garlic is often called for.

There are myriad garlic presses, crushers and mincers out there to help you in this task. Their popularity is partly to do with people wishing to avoid their hands smelling of garlic, as well as their ease and speed of use. One way to get rid of the smell is simply to rub your hands on something made of stainless steel. It is possible to buy odour-removing stainless steel 'soap' bars specifically for this purpose.

Against garlic crushers is the fact that cleaning some of these gizmos can be fiddly and, all too often, pieces of garlic are left behind in the gadget. An easy, gadget-free way of crushing garlic, favoured by many chefs, is to place a peeled, chopped clove on a chopping board, sprinkle over a pinch of salt (which helps break it down), cover it with the broad side of a large knife, then press down hard repeatedly onto the blade, crushing the garlic into a paste.

When buying garlic, choose heads that are firm and plump, avoiding any that look dried out and shrivelled. The best way of storing garlic is to keep it in dry, cool and, ideally, dark conditions, for example, in a basket, ceramic pot or a breathable mesh bag inside a cupboard. Storing garlic in the fridge encourages it to sprout and is not advised. Usefully, whole garlic heads and loose garlic cloves stored correctly will keep well for several weeks. The majority of garlic we buy has already been allowed to dry out after harvesting by the growers. An exception to this is new-season 'wet garlic' (sometimes called green garlic), which is freshly harvested. Try and use this as soon as possible before it begins to dry out.

One traditional way of storing garlic is in plaits or braids, and garlic farms often sell their wares in this form. These are generally made by the garlic growers themselves from softneck garlic, using the long stalks of the garlic to plait/braid the heads together once it has been dried. Appealingly rustic, a plait/braid of garlic hung from a hook in the kitchen out of direct light is picturesque and allows for air to circulate and keep the garlic dry.

Garlic can be frozen peeled or unpeeled, as whole cloves, chopped, or in paste form. If freezing, bear in mind that the odour can permeate other ingredients, so be sure to store it in a well-sealed container or wrap it in a couple of layers of plastic sandwich bags, clingfilm/plastic wrap or parchment paper.

A delicious way of preserving the flavour of garlic is to make garlic-infused oil. While this is a straightforward process, a few simple but important steps need to be followed to make it correctly and safely and prevent any toxins from forming. Fry the garlic cloves gently in a little olive oil, stirring them often to prevent them browning, for around 3 minutes until fragrant. Add in the remaining olive oil for the quantity required to the pan and simmer for 20 minutes. Strain the oil well, allow to cool and pour into a dry, sterilized glass bottle. Store in the fridge and consume within a week.

It is also possible to infuse vinegar with garlic. Use a good quality vinegar and be sure to check the label to ensure that the vinegar has an acetic acid content of at least 5 per cent (which makes it hard for micro-organisms to survive) and for best results heat the vinegar before steeping the garlic.

Hummus

This tasty, nutty-flavoured Middle Eastern dip is so easy to make at home. Serve it with pitta bread, falafel or vegetable crudités as a snack or alongside other mezze dishes for a light meal.

125 g/¾ cup dried chickpeas/garbanzo beans
1 teaspoon bicarbonate of soda/baking soda
2 garlic cloves, crushed to a paste
4 tablespoons tahini
freshly squeezed juice of 1 lemon
salt

TO GARNISH
olive oil
paprika or sumac
finely chopped fresh parsley

Serves 6

Soak the chickpeas/garbanzo beans overnight in plenty of cold water with the bicarbonate of soda/baking soda.

Next day, drain and rinse. Place in a large pan, add enough fresh cold water to cover well and bring to the boil. Reduce the heat and simmer for 50–60 minutes until tender, skimming off any scum. Season the chickpeas with salt, then drain, reserving the cooking water and setting aside 1 tablespoon of the cooked chickpeas/garbanzo beans for the garnish.

In a food processor, blend together the cooked chickpeas/garbanzo beans, garlic, tahini and lemon juice. Gradually add in the cooking liquid until the mixture becomes a smooth paste. Season with salt.

Transfer the hummus to a serving bowl. To serve, make a shallow hollow in the centre using the back of a spoon. Pour in a little olive oil, top with the reserved whole chickpeas/garbanzo beans and sprinkle with paprika and parsley.

Bean and garlic dip

A fresh-tasting dip, with a pleasant nutty flavour.
Serve with pitta bread or crudités.

250 g/9 oz. frozen broad/fava
   beans
2 roast garlic cloves
   (see page 23),
   peeled and mashed
1 tablespoon olive oil
100 g/½ cup ricotta cheese

2 tablespoons chopped fresh
   dill, plus fronds to garnish
salt and freshly ground black
   pepper

Serves 4

Cook the frozen beans in a saucepan of boiling water until just tender. Drain, cool and pop the beans out of their tough skins.

Place the skinned beans, roast garlic and olive oil in a food processor and blend together; alternatively mash together in a bowl using a fork. Add in the ricotta, chopped dill, salt and pepper and blend together briefly.

Cover and chill. To serve, garnish with dill fronds.

Roast garlic beetroot/beet soup

2 garlic cloves,
    unpeeled
500 g/1 lb. 2 oz. raw
    beetroot/beets
1 tablespoon olive oil
½ onion, finely chopped
a splash of red wine
    (optional)
600 ml/2½ cups fresh
    chicken or vegetable
    stock
salt and freshly ground
    black pepper
crème fraîche or sour
    cream, to serve
chopped tarragon, to
    serve

Serves 4

This striking soup has a pleasantly earthy sweetness to it. Serve as a hearty appetizer or for a light lunch, with some good crusty bread on the side.

Preheat the oven to 200°C (400°F) Gas 6.

Cut the tip off each unpeeled garlic clove, to just expose the clove inside. Wrap the garlic and beetroot/beets together in foil, sealing well. Place on a baking sheet and bake in the preheated oven for 1 hour. Unwrap and set aside to cool.

Peel the beetroot/beets and roughly chop. Peel the garlic and mash it.

Next, heat the oil in a large saucepan set over a low heat. Add the onion and fry gently until softened. Add the chopped beetroot/beets, mashed garlic and a splash of red wine if desired. Cook for 2 minutes, then pour in the stock. Bring to the boil, cover, reduce the heat and simmer for 30 minutes.

Leave to cool a little, then blend until smooth, using a stick blender or a food processor. Season with salt and pepper, return to the pan and gently heat through.

To serve, pour into bowls and garnish with crème fraîche or sour cream and chopped tarragon.

Pan-fried gnocchi with garlic mushrooms and pancetta

A hearty, rustic dish, perfect for a comforting supper after a busy day. Use as many different mushrooms as you can find for a range of flavours and textures. When in season, a few wild mushrooms would add a touch of luxury.

500 g/1 lb. 2 oz. potato
   gnocchi
2 tablespoons olive oil
50 g/2 oz. pancetta, diced
2 garlic cloves, chopped
a sprig of fresh thyme
500 g/1 lb. 2 oz. assorted
   mushrooms (such as
   button, oyster and
   shiitake), small ones
   left whole, large ones
   roughly sliced
25 g/1 oz. dried and chopped
   porcini mushrooms,
   soaked in hot water for
   15 minutes, then drained
a splash of dry white wine
freshly grated nutmeg
15 g/1 tablespoon butter
salt and freshly ground black
   pepper
chopped fresh parsley,
   to garnish
grated Parmesan cheese,
   to serve

Serves 4

Boil the gnocchi in a large pan of boiling salted water until cooked (check packet intructions for cooking time); drain and set aside.

Heat 1 tablespoon of the olive oil in large frying pan/skillet. Add the pancetta, garlic and thyme and fry, stirring often, for 2 minutes. Add the assorted mushrooms and porcini, mixing in well. Add the wine and cook, stirring, until evaporated. Season with salt, pepper and nutmeg and fry, stirring often, until the mushrooms are cooked through but retain their texture. Set aside.

In a separate large frying pan/skillet, heat the remaining olive oil and the butter. Once the mixture is frothing, add the cooked gnocchi, spreading them out in a single layer. Fry for a few minutes, turning now and then, until golden brown on all sides. Add the fried mushroom mixture, mixing it in well, and cook until the mushrooms are heated through.

Garnish with the parsley and serve at once with grated Parmesan cheese to sprinkle over.

Roast garlic crab tart

A rich treat of a savoury tart, studded with mellow roast garlic cloves. Serve with a refreshing fennel and watercress salad, for a pleasing contrast of textures.

250 g/9 oz. shortcrust
  pastry/pie dough
2 eggs plus 1 egg yolk,
  beaten together
300 ml/1¼ cups crème
  fraîche or double/heavy
  cream
a pinch of saffron threads,
  finely ground and soaked
  in 1 teaspoon hot water
250 g/9½ oz. picked crab
  meat (white and brown)
8 roast garlic cloves
  (see page 23), peeled,
  left whole
salt and freshly ground
  black pepper

*22-cm/9-in. loose-based
  tart pan, greased*

baking beans

Serves 6–8

Preheat the oven to 200°C (400°F) Gas 6.

Roll out the pastry/pie dough thinly and use it to line the greased tart pan. Line the pastry case with a square of parchment paper, then fill with baking beans.

Blind bake the pastry case in the preheated oven for 10 minutes. Remove the parchment paper and beans and bake uncovered for a further 5 minutes. Brush a little of the beaten eggs over the case and bake for a further 5 minutes. Remove from the oven, leaving it on at 200°C (400°F) Gas 6.

Meanwhile, prepare the filling. Whisk the crème fraîche or cream with the beaten eggs. Stir in the saffron liquid. Season with salt and pepper.

Spread the crab meat evenly in the part-baked pastry case. Dot over the roast garlic cloves. Pour over the crème fraîche/egg mixture.

Bake in the preheated oven for 30–40 minutes. Remove and serve warm or cool.

Roast garlic salt cod croquettes

These crisp, light-textured croquettes, with their subtle, salty, fishy flavour, are addictively good! Serve with either the parsley pesto or the roast garlic tartare sauce. Great with a crisp side salad for a light meal or enjoy as a snack.

1 head of garlic

600 g/1 lb. 5 oz. salt cod fillet, soaked for 24 hours, with water changed 2–3 times during soaking period

600 g/1 lb. 5 oz. floury potatoes, such as King Edwards, peeled and chopped

2 eggs, lightly beaten

2 tablespoons freshly chopped parsley

grated zest of 1 lemon

oil, for deep-frying

salt

PARSLEY PESTO
50 g/2 cups freshly chopped parsley

120 ml/½ cup olive oil

salt

ROAST GARLIC TARTARE SAUCE
200 g/1 cup mayonnaise

2 tablespoons finely chopped gherkins

1 tablespoon capers

2 roast garlic cloves, peeled and mashed (taken from head used in croquettes above)

2 tablespoons finely chopped fresh parsley

Makes 24 croquettes (serves 4–6 for a light lunch)

To roast the garlic, preheat the oven to 180°C (350°F) Gas 4.

Slice the top off the garlic head, to expose the cloves inside. Wrap in foil and bake the garlic head in the preheated oven for 1 hour. Unwrap the foil and set the garlic head aside to cool.

When the garlic is cool enough to handle, squeeze out the softened roast garlic from each clove. Set aside and then mash 4 cloves for the croquettes and 2 cloves for the tartare sauce.

To make the croquettes, drain the soaked salt cod and place in a pan. Cover generously with cold water, bring to the boil and cook over a medium heat until tender, around 20 minutes; drain.

Boil the potatoes in salted water until tender; drain, mash and allow to cool. Mix the 4 mashed roast garlic cloves into the potatoes.

When the salt cod is cool enough to handle, use your fingers to go through it and discard any skin and bones. Flake the fish.

In a large bowl, mix together the flaked salt cod, mashed potato, eggs, parsley and lemon zest, mixing well. Using 2 tablespoons, shape the mixture into 24 croquettes and set aside to cool completely.

If serving with parsley pesto, blitz together the parsley and olive oil in a food processor, then season with salt.

If serving with roast garlic tartare sauce, simply mix all the ingredients together and chill before serving. (This tartare sauce is also good with fish and chips, or fish-finger/fish stick sandwiches.)

Heat the oil for deep-frying in a large saucepan until very hot. Fry the croquettes in batches until a rich golden brown in colour, turning them over during frying so that they brown on both sides. Remove and drain on kitchen paper.

Serve warm from frying or at room temperature with the parsley pesto or roast garlic tartare sauce on the side.

Flowering Chinese chive prawns/shrimp

Flowering Chinese chives are a lesser-known variety of Chinese chives, both can be found in Chinese stores/supermarkets. Either would work well in this recipe, providing a subtle garlic flavour and pleasant texture. Serve with noodles for a quick and tasty meal.

1 tablespoon sunflower or
    vegetable oil
2 cm/¾ in. fresh ginger,
    peeled and finely sliced
200 g/7 oz. flowering
    Chinese chives or
    Chinese chives, chopped
    into 2.5-cm/1-in. lengths
200 g/7 oz. raw
    prawns/shrimp, peeled

1 tablespoon rice wine
    or medium sherry
1 tablespoon light soy
    sauce
½ teaspoon sesame oil

Serves 2

Place the oil in a wok over a high heat. Add the ginger and stir-fry until fragrant. Next put in the Chinese chives and stir-fry briefly.

Add the prawns/shrimp and stir-fry. As soon as the prawns/shrimp turn opaque, add the rice wine and sizzle briefly. Lastly, throw in the soy sauce and sesame oil. Stir-fry for 2–3 minutes until Chinese chives are just wilted. Serve at once.

Chicken with 40 cloves of garlic

Yes, this is truly a dish for garlic lovers! Pot-roasting the bird makes for tender, flavourful chicken, aromatic with tarragon. Serve the cooked whole garlic cloves with the chicken so that guests can squeeze the softened garlic out of the skins as a rich and tasty accompaniment.

1.8 kg/4 lb. free-range chicken
25 g/1½ tablespoons butter
1 tablespoon olive oil
40 garlic cloves, separated but unpeeled
100 ml/⅓ cup vermouth or dry white wine
freshly squeezed juice of ½ lemon
200 ml/1 cup good-quality chicken stock

a handful of fresh tarragon sprigs
salt and freshly ground black pepper

a lidded flameproof casserole dish, large enough to hold the chicken

Serves 6

Preheat the oven to 180°C (350°F) Gas 4.

Season the chicken with salt and pepper. Heat the butter and olive oil in a large frying pan/skillet. Add the chicken and brown on all sides. Save the pan juices.

Meanwhile, heat the casserole dish on the stovetop. Transfer the browned chicken to the casserole dish. Tuck some of the garlic cloves into the cavity, sprinkle the rest around the chicken and pour over the vermouth or wine. Allow to sizzle briefly, then pour in the buttery juices from the frying pan/skillet, the lemon juice and stock. Add the tarragon, placing a few sprigs inside the cavity.

Bring to the boil on the stovetop, then cover with the lid and transfer the casserole to the preheated oven. Bake, covered, for 1 hour 20 minutes–1 hour 30 minutes until the chicken is cooked through and the juices run clear.

Transfer the chicken to a serving dish. Use a slotted spoon to transfer the garlic cloves to the dish. Pour the juices into a serving jug/pitcher to use as a gravy, skimming off any excess fat. Serve the chicken with the garlic cloves and gravy.

Smoked garlic pulled pork

Slow-cooked, tender pork with its smoky garlicky flavour is a tasty dish, contrasting well with this tangy dressing. Serve the shredded pork in bread rolls or as a buffet dish with potato salad and coleslaw.

2.2-kg/5-lb. pork shoulder on the bone, skin scored for crackling
2 smoked garlic cloves, thinly sliced
2 teaspoons smoked garlic powder
2 tablespoons olive oil
8 bread rolls
salt and freshly ground black pepper

DRESSING
6 tablespoons red wine vinegar
2 tablespoons clear honey
2 roast garlic cloves (see page 23), peeled and mashed
salt

Serves 8

Preheat the oven to 220°C (425°F) Gas 7. Bring the pork to room temperature.

Pat the pork dry with paper towels and season the skin thoroughly with salt. Lightly score the flesh, then cut small incisions and insert the chopped smoked garlic pieces. Season the flesh with smoked garlic powder, salt and freshly ground black pepper.

Line a large roasting pan with a large piece of foil. Place the pork in the middle of the foil, pour over the olive oil, then wrap the foil up over the pork to form a parcel.

Roast for 15 minutes in the preheated oven, then reduce the temperature to 150°C (300°F) Gas 2. Cook the pork for a further 5 hours 45 minutes.

Unwrap the pork, saving the pan juices. Discard any fat, or if you want crispy crackling, remove the fat and place under a hot grill/broiler for 10–15 minutes. Using two forks, pull the soft cooked pork off the bone in long shreds. Toss the pulled pork with 3–4 tablespoons of the roasting pan juices for extra moisture.

Mix together the dressing ingredients and season to taste.

Fill the rolls generously with pulled pork, topping with the tangy dressing as required.

Garlicky goose fat roast potatoes

Everybody loves roast potatoes and these ones are irresistibly moreish. Serve with roast beef, lamb, pork or chicken.

1 tablespoon goose fat
a pinch of salt
700 g/1½ lbs. roasting potatoes, peeled and cut into large, even chunks
8 garlic cloves, unpeeled
sea salt flakes

Serves 4
as a side dish

Preheat the oven to 220°C (425°F) Gas 7. Place the goose fat in a roasting pan and preheat in the oven.

Bring a large pan of salted water to the boil. Add the potatoes and cook for 10 minutes to par-boil them; drain, return to the pan and shake to roughen their surface.

Add the par-boiled potatoes to the hot goose fat in the roasting pan, shaking to coat them well. Sprinkle in the garlic cloves and season with salt flakes. Roast for 30–40 minutes, turning over now and then to brown on all sides, until golden brown. Serve at once.

Italian-style garlic spinach

An elegant and easy vegetable dish, this garlicky spinach makes the perfect accompaniment for roast lamb or beef.

500 g/1 lb. fresh large leaf spinach, rinsed
2 tablespoons olive oil
1 garlic clove, peeled and left whole
a squeeze of fresh lemon juice
salt and freshly ground black pepper

Serves 4
as a side dish

Place the spinach in a large, heavy-based pan and season with salt. Cover and cook for a few minutes until the spinach has just wilted (no need to add extra water). Drain in a colander, pressing with a spatula to squeeze out excess moisture. Roughly chop.

Heat the oil in a large frying pan/skillet. Add the garlic and fry, stirring, until browned on all sides; remove and discard the garlic. Add the chopped spinach to the pan and fry in the garlic oil, turning to coat thoroughly. Season to taste, add a squeeze of lemon juice and serve at once.

Sunshine garlic

Garlic for health

Historically, human beings have had a very special relationship with garlic (*Allium sativum*). Not only has it been relished for its ability to add bold flavour to food but also as a traditional medicine attributed with numerous special healing powers. For centuries, doctors and alternative health practitioners have treated the natural world as a medicine chest, searching for remedies and using plants, including garlic, to treat illnesses.

Garlic is particularly striking because of the range of ailments it has been used to treat. Used both internally and externally, it has been prescribed raw, prepared in food, taken with vinegar or wine, applied to wounds in the form of poultices, rubbed on bruises or mixed with goose fat and applied to ears.

In Indian Ayurvedic medicine, garlic is highly valued, used as a diuretic, as a pick-me-up, to aid digestion and to treat heart disease and arthritis.

In Chinese medicine, garlic was considered as a stimulant and warmer (yang in the yin–and–yang view of the universe) and used to help relieve depression. The Ancient Egyptians used garlic as a fortifying medicine, with the slaves who built the pyramids given daily doses of garlic in order to keep them strong. This perception of it as a strengthening food continued with the Greeks and Romans, with garlic fed to Olympian athletes and soldiers. In Ancient Greece, Hippocrates (460–370 BC), the renowned physician, recommended garlic in treating pneumonia and other infections. The Roman author and naturalist Pliny the Elder (AD 23–AD 79) wrote that 'garlic has powerful properties', advising that it can be used to treat snake bites, applied to bruises and taken to induce sleep.

Through the centuries, garlic has continued to be valued in many countries for its healthy properties. In Europe during the Middle Ages, garlic was used to treat digestive disorders, constipation and the plague. The sixteenth-century Italian physician Pietro Andrea Mattioli (1501–1577) recommended that garlic be used to treat digestive disorders and worms. In nineteenth-century America, John Gunn's *Home Book of Health* recommended that garlic be used to treat asthma, lung disorders and infections. In Russia garlic was widely used to treat respiratory tract diseases.

As our scientific knowledge of plants and their medicinal properties has progressed, so has our understanding of garlic's antibacterial powers. In 1858 the French scientist Louis Pasteur experimented with garlic and noted its ability to destroy bacteria. Throughout World War I, garlic was used to dress wounds and during World War II, with conventional medicines in short supply, garlic was used instead by the Red Army to treat soldiers in Russia, hence its nickname 'Russian penicillin'.

Our age-old fascination with garlic as a healthy food shows no signs of abating. We now know that garlic contains the compound alliin and the enzyme alliinase which, when garlic is cut or crushed, come together to create allicin. This compound allicin (incidentally responsible for garlic's odour) is known to have antibacterial and antifungal medicinal properties.

Garlic also contains ajoene, which functions as an antioxidant and also has antithrombotic properties which helps to prevent blood clots from forming.

Garlic is recognized by medical authorities as reducing lipids (fats) in our blood, specifically cholesterol. When it comes to cardiovascular health, garlic's sulphur-containing compounds are thought to protect against inflammation and oxidative stress.

Garlic and garlic products are still widely prescribed around the world to treat a range of conditions. Scientific research continues to explore its health-giving properties, among them the potential it may have as a cancer-fighting anticarcinogen.

Roast garlic herbed labneh

Making labneh (also labne, labni or yogurt cheese) is very simple, but do bear in mind that it takes 24 hours to strain the yogurt. Serve this Middle Eastern cheese as an appetizer with vegetable crudités and hot pitta bread.

450 g/2 cups full-fat
  goat's milk yogurt
salt
2 roast garlic cloves
  (see page 23)
finely grated zest of
  1 lemon
3 tablespoons finely
  chopped fresh parsley
1 teaspoon finely
  chopped fresh chives
1 teaspoon fresh thyme
  leaves
olive oil, to serve
pistachio nuts, finely
  ground, to garnish

*a muslin/cheesecloth
  square and string*

Serve 4-6

First, make the labneh. Season the yogurt with salt to taste, mixing it in well. Place the yogurt in the centre of the muslin/cheesecloth square, fold up the muslin/cheesecloth around the yogurt and tie tightly, forming a parcel. Suspend the muslin/cheesecloth parcel over a deep, large bowl by tying it with the string to a wooden spoon laid across the top of the bowl.

Leave in the fridge for 24 hours, during which time the excess moisture will drip out of the parcel.

Squeeze the roast garlic out of the papery skin and mash into a paste. Flavour the labneh by mixing it with the roast garlic, lemon zest, parsley, chives and thyme.

Transfer the labneh to a serving dish. Use the back of a spoon to make a little hollow in the middle of the labneh, pour in a little olive oil, sprinkle with ground pistachio nuts and serve.

Roast garlic rosemary focaccia

Freshly made focaccia is always a treat, with roast garlic adding a wonderful savouriness and rosemary an appealing aromatic note. Serve on its own or with Italian charcuterie, such as parma ham/prosciutto or mortadella, for a light meal.

500 g/3½ cups strong white bread flour, plus extra for dusting

1 teaspoon fast-action dried yeast

1 teaspoon salt

1 teaspoon sugar

300 ml/1¼ cups hand-hot water

5 tablespoons extra virgin olive oil

6 roast garlic cloves (see page 23), peeled and chopped

3 tablespoons rosemary leaves, finely chopped

a pinch of sea salt flakes

a large mixing bowl, oiled

a baking sheet, greased

Makes 1 loaf; serves 6

Mix together the flour, yeast, salt and sugar. Gradually add in the water and 2 tablespoons of the oil, bringing the mixture together to form a sticky dough. Turn out onto a lightly floured surface and knead until smooth and elastic. Then work in the roast garlic and 2 tablespoons of the rosemary. Transfer to the prepared mixing bowl, cover with a clean damp kitchen cloth and set aside in a warm place to rise for 1 hour.

Break down the risen dough and shape into a large oval on the prepared baking sheet.

Using your fingertips, press into the dough to make numerous small indentations. Spoon over 2 tablespoons of the oil, so that it fills the indents, and sprinkle over the remaining rosemary. Set aside to rest for 30 minutes.

Preheat the oven to 200°C (400°F) Gas 6.

Bake the focaccia in the preheated oven until golden brown. Spoon over the remaining oil and sprinkle with the sea salt flakes.

Serve warm from the oven or at room temperature.

Green garlic muffins

1 teaspoon olive oil

2 garlic cloves, chopped

225 g/1¾ cups self-raising/self-rising flour

1 teaspoon baking powder

1 teaspoon salt

1 egg

50 g/4 tablespoons natural yogurt

100–125 ml/⅓–½ cup whole milk

150 g/1¾ cups grated courgettes/zucchini

50 g/½ cup chopped pistachio nuts

50 g/½ cup grated Cheddar cheese

a 12-hole muffin pan, lined with paper cases

Makes 12

These tasty muffins, flecked with grated courgette/zucchini and chopped pistachio nuts, are great for brunch; serve warm from the oven with butter or cream cheese.

Heat the oil in a small frying pan/skillet and gently fry the garlic until golden, stirring and taking care not to burn it. Set aside to cool.

Preheat the oven to 200°C (400°F) Gas 6.

Sift the flour, baking powder and salt into a mixing bowl. In a separate bowl, whisk together the egg, yogurt and 100 ml/⅓ cup milk. Pour the egg mixture over the sifted ingredients and stir together, taking care not to over-mix. If the mixture appears very dry then add the extra milk. Fold in the fried garlic, grated courgette/zucchini, chopped pistachios and grated Cheddar.

Divide the mixture among the muffin cases. Bake in the preheated oven for 20 minutes until risen and golden brown. Serve warm from the oven or allow to cool.

Ajo blanco

Also known as white gazpacho, this classic Spanish cold soup, simply made from a few humble ingredients, has a delicate nutty flavour. Garnished, as is traditional, with fresh grapes or melon, it makes a visually appealing and refreshing first course or light lunch.

100 g/3½ oz. slightly stale white bread, crusts trimmed, sliced

700 ml/3 cups cold water

200 g/1½ cups blanched almonds

2 garlic cloves, crushed

6 tablespoons extra virgin olive oil, plus extra for serving

2 tablespoons sherry vinegar

salt

24 white seedless grapes, halved, or 200 g/7 oz. green or orange melon, cut into small chunks

Serves 4

Soak the bread in the cold water for 30 minutes until softened.

Finely grind the almonds in a food processor. Add the soaked bread and half the soaking water, reserving the remainder. Blitz until smooth. Add the crushed garlic, olive oil and sherry vinegar and blend together until smooth.

Add in enough of the remaining soaking water to give the soup a creamy texture. Season with salt. Cover and chill in the fridge for at least 2–3 hours.

Serve garnished with a drizzle of olive oil and grape halves or small chunks of melon.

Black garlic tricolore salad

Insalata tricolore — Italy's patriotic red, white and green salad — is a classic which, when made with good-quality tomatoes, ripe avocado and fresh mozzarella, is such a treat to eat. Adding black garlic is an unorthodox touch, but the smoky sweetness of black garlic works well with the balsamic vinegar and gives an interesting flavour to the dish.

6 tablespoons extra virgin olive oil

2 tablespoons balsamic vinegar

2 black garlic cloves, finely chopped

3 mozzarella cheese balls, drained and sliced

4 ripe tomatoes, sliced

2 avocados, sliced and tossed with a little lemon juice to prevent discolouring

a handful of fresh basil leaves

salt and freshly ground black pepper

Serves 4

Make the dressing by placing the olive oil, balsamic vinegar and black garlic in a small lidded jar, then shaking well to mix together. Season with salt and pepper.

Arrange the mozzarella, tomato and avocado in overlapping slices on a large serving plate. Pour over the black garlic dressing, scatter over the basil leaves and serve at once.

Thai prawn/shrimp pomelo salad with garlic and herb dressing

Pomelo is a thick-skinned citrus fruit with a distinctive flavour and juicy texture. It is often used in Thai salads. The contrast in textures works well, with the tasty dressing adding a pleasant piquant punch. If pomelo is unavailable, white grapefruit can be used instead.

½ pomelo, or
  1 grapefruit
1 ripe mango
200 g/7 oz. cooked, peeled king
  prawns/jumbo shrimp

DRESSING
15 g/1 cup fresh
  coriander/cilantro leaves
10 g/⅔ cup fresh mint leaves
1 garlic clove, peeled

1 green chilli/chile, chopped
grated zest of ½ lime
freshly squeezed juice of 1 lime
a pinch of salt

*Serves 4 as
an appetizer or
2 as a light meal*

Make the herb dressing by blitzing together the coriander/cilantro, mint, garlic, chilli/chile, lime zest, lime juice and salt into a paste in a food processor.

Peel the pomelo half and separate into segments. Peel each segment of its tough skin and slice into pieces.

Using a sharp knife, halve the mango, discarding the large central stone. Cut a criss-cross pattern across each mango cheek, then cut out the mango chunks, discarding the skin.

Toss together the pomelo, mango and prawns/shrimp with the herb dressing, mixing well. Serve at once or cover and chill until serving.

Spaghetti alle vongole

One for shellfish lovers, this simple yet classic pasta dish offers a taste of the sea, Italian style. Fresh clams have a distinctive sweetness and texture, flavoured here simply but effectively with olive oil, garlic, white wine and parsley.

1 kg/2 lb. 3 oz. fresh
    clams
400 g/14 oz. spaghetti
6 tablespoons olive oil
3 garlic cloves, finely
    sliced lengthways
6 tablespoons finely
    chopped fresh parsley
100 ml/⅓ cup dry white
    wine
salt and freshly ground
    black pepper

Serves 4

Prepare the clams by rinsing them under running water and sorting through, discarding any that are open. Keep in the fridge until you are ready to cook them.

Bring a large pan of salted water to the boil. Add the spaghetti and cook until al dente; drain.

Meanwhile, heat the olive oil in a large saucepan. Add the garlic and fry gently until just golden, stirring often. Take care not to burn the garlic, as this would give a bitter flavour. Add the clams, 2 tablespoons of the chopped parsley and the white wine.

Cover and cook for a few minutes until the clams have opened. Discard any that remain closed. Season with pepper.

Toss together the cooked spaghetti, clams and remaining parsley, adding just enough of the clam cooking liquor to moisten the spaghetti. Serve at once.

Spanish garlic prawns/shrimp

This quick-to-cook classic tapas dish, made from a few simple ingredients including garlic and smoked Spanish paprika, is addictively moreish. Cook and serve it at once as a first course or as part of a tapas feast. Do make sure you have plenty of bread on hand for soaking up the flavourful olive oil.

4 tablespoons olive oil
2 garlic cloves, chopped
2 small dried red chillies/chiles, crumbled
450 g/1 lb. raw prawns/shrimp, peeled, deveined, rinsed and dried
1 teaspoon sweet smoked Spanish paprika
1 tablespoon finely chopped fresh parsley
salt
crusty bread, to serve

Serves 4 as a tapas dish

Heat the olive oil in a heavy-based frying pan/skillet. Add the chopped garlic and fry briefly, stirring, until fragrant. Add the crumbled chillies/chiles, mixing well, then add the prawns/shrimp, mixing to coat them in the oil.

Fry the prawns/shrimp briefly, stirring, until they turn opaque and pink on both sides, taking care not to over-cook them and dry them out. Season with salt, then add the Spanish paprika, mixing in. Sprinkle with parsley and serve at once with crusty bread.

Garlic lime chicken

Flavoured with plenty of lime zest and juice, this is a true sunshine recipe, which would be perfect for a barbecue on a hot summer's day. Serve with griddled pineapple, a herby rice salad and an ice-cold mojito or margarita on the side.

4 garlic cloves, crushed
grated zest and freshly squeezed
   juice of 2 limes
2 tablespoons olive oil
2 tablespoons light soy sauce

2 teaspoons brown sugar
8 chicken thighs, bone in, skin on
salt and freshly ground black pepper

Serves 4

Mix together the garlic, lime juice and zest, olive oil, soy sauce and sugar to form a marinade. Season the chicken with salt and pepper, then place in a non-metallic bowl. Toss with the marinade, coating well. Cover and marinate in the fridge for 4 hours or overnight.

Fire up the barbecue or preheat the oven to 200°C (400°F) Gas 6.

Place the thighs on a rack in a tray and roast in the oven for 25–30 minutes or until cooked through. Alternatively cook the chicken on the barbecue, turning occasionally, until the juices run clear and the skin is nicely browned. Serve at once with griddled pineapple and herby rice salad.

Saffron garlic chicken kebabs/kabobs

Marinating chicken is a simple but effective way of adding flavour. These kebabs/kabobs would also be great for a barbecue. Serve with basmati rice, the Tzatziki dip (below) or a raita and a side salad.

a generous pinch of saffron threads

2 garlic cloves

3 tablespoons olive oil, plus extra for basting

freshly squeezed juice of ½ lemon

500 g/1 lb. 2 oz. chicken breast fillet, cut into approx. 2.5-cm/1-inch cubes

salt

torn fresh mint leaves, to garnish

8 wooden skewers, soaked in water

Serves 4

Grind the saffron threads, then soak in 1 teaspoon of warm water.

Pound the garlic into a paste and mix with a pinch of salt.

Mix together the garlic, saffron water, olive oil, lemon juice and salt in a large bowl to make the marinade. Add the chicken and toss, coating thoroughly in the marinade. Cover and marinate in the fridge for 4–6 hours, turning over the chicken pieces halfway through.

Preheat the grill/broiler until very hot. Thread the marinated chicken onto the skewers, dividing the pieces evenly.

Grill the chicken kebabs/kabobs for about 15 minutes until cooked through and the juices run clear, turning often and basting with a little oil if required. Serve at once, garnished with torn fresh mint.

Tzatziki

This delicate, refreshing and garlicky Greek dip is a classic. Serve with the chicken kebabs/kabobs or with pitta bread or crudités for a snack.

½ cucumber

1 garlic clove, crushed

250 g/1½ cups Greek yogurt

1 tablespoon chopped fresh mint leaves

1 tablespoon olive oil

1 teaspoon white wine vinegar

salt

Serves 6

Peel the cucumber and grate it.

Sprinkle with salt and set aside for 15 minutes to draw out moisture; drain and pat dry with paper towels.

Mix together the grated cucumber, garlic, yogurt, chopped mint, olive oil and vinegar. Cover and chill until ready to serve.

Roast garlic pork burgers

Making your own burgers is very simple and allows you to be creative with the flavourings. Adding roast garlic, fennel seeds and lemon zest gives a great depth of flavour to these tasty burgers, perfect for summertime barbecues. Serve with fries and crunchy coleslaw.

½ teaspoon fennel seeds
1 roasted head of garlic
(see page 23)
400 g/14 oz. minced/
ground pork
1 tablespoon finely
chopped fresh parsley
1 teaspoon grated lemon
zest
sunflower or vegetable
oil, for frying
salt and freshly ground
black pepper
4 brioche rolls or
hamburger buns
mayonnaise, ketchup
and sliced gherkins,
as desired

Serves 4

Dry-fry the fennel seeds in a frying pan/skillet until fragrant, then cool and grind.

When the roasted garlic is cool enough to handle, squeeze out the softened pulp from each clove and mash into a paste.

Mix together the minced/ground pork, roast garlic paste, ground fennel, parsley and lemon zest, mixing thoroughly. Season well with salt and pepper. Shape the minced/ground pork into 4 patties.

Add a touch of oil to a large frying pan/skillet and heat through. Add the patties and fry for 15–20 minutes, or until cooked through, turning over as they cook.

Place the patties in the rolls, adding mayonnaise, ketchup and gherkins to taste and serve at once.

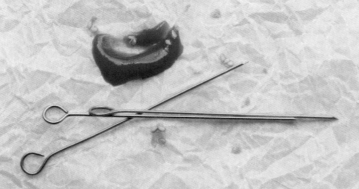

Garlic pilaf

Fragrant basmati rice, cooked with herbs and spices in chicken stock, becomes a tasty and elegant rice dish. This makes an excellent accompaniment to curries and meat or chicken dishes, such as the Saffron Garlic Chicken Kebabs/Kabobs (see page 55) and Fragrant Garlic Lamb Shanks with Apricots (see page 152).

250 g/1¼ cups basmati rice
1 tablespoon olive oil
1 garlic clove, chopped
1 bay leaf
½ cinnamon stick
10 g/2 teaspoons butter
300 ml/1¼ cups chicken stock or water
a good pinch of saffron strands, finely ground and soaked with 1 tablespoon hot water
salt
1 tablespoon pine nuts, toasted
1 tablespoon finely chopped fresh parsley

Serves 4

Rinse the basmati thoroughly in cold running water to wash out the excess starch; drain well.

Heat the olive oil in a small, heavy-based saucepan. Add the garlic and fry, stirring, until golden. Take care not to burn it, as it would become bitter. Add the bay leaf and cinnamon stick, then stir in the butter until it has melted.

Add the rice, mixing well to coat thoroughly in the oil/butter. Add the stock, saffron water and salt to taste.

Bring to the boil, then reduce the heat to very low, cover and cook for 15–20 minutes until the water has been absorbed and the rice is soft and fluffy. Discard the bay leaf and cinnamon stick. Sprinkle over the pine nuts and parsley and serve at once.

Garlic and almond purple sprouting broccoli

Cooking purple sprouting broccoli in this way retains its crunchy texture, while giving it a boost in the flavour stakes. Serve as a side dish alongside Garlic Butter Roast Chicken (see page 82) or with Garlic Anchovy Roast Lamb (see page 155), or toss with cooked pasta for a vegetarian meal.

300 g/10½ oz. purple sprouting broccoli, chopped into 2.5-cm/1-in. lengths, or broccoli florets
25 g/⅓ cup flaked/slivered almonds
2 tablespoons olive oil
1 large garlic clove, roughly chopped
salt and freshly ground black pepper

Serves 4

Bring a large pan of salted water to the boil. Add the broccoli and cook for 2 minutes, then drain thoroughly and refresh in cold water to stop the cooking process.

Dry-fry the almonds in a frying pan/skillet, stirring often, until golden brown; set aside.

Heat the olive oil in a large frying pan/skillet. Add the garlic and fry until golden and fragrant. Add the drained broccoli and fry briefly for 2 minutes, stirring to coat it in the oil. Add the almonds, season with freshly ground pepper and serve at once.

Garlic peas a la Française

This can be made with fresh peas and freshly harvested, new season wet garlic, but it works equally well with frozen peas and garlic. Serve as a vegetable side dish – it goes particularly well with roast lamb.

15 g/1 tablespoon butter
2 spring onions/scallions, chopped into 1-cm/½-in. pieces
1 rasher/slice bacon, chopped into strips
2 wet (or green) garlic cloves (or 1 garlic clove), chopped
75 g/2 cups lettuce leaves, such as Little Gem, shredded
400 g/3 cups fresh or frozen peas
150 ml/⅔ cup chicken or vegetable stock
salt and freshly ground black pepper

Serves 4

Melt the butter in a heavy-based saucepan. Add the spring onions/scallions, bacon and garlic and fry, stirring, for 2 minutes until the mixture smells fragrant and the bacon has turned opaque. Add the lettuce, peas and stock and season with salt and pepper. Bring to the boil, cover and cook for 5 minutes until the peas are tender.

Serve with the cooking juices, so it has an almost soupy texture.

Comfort garlic

Garlic folklore

Fascinatingly, this everyday ingredient has long been linked with magic, myths, folklore and superstitions. The association is closely intertwined with its historic reputation as a plant with health-giving properties (see page 34). In many cultures, garlic was traditionally thought to endow warriors with strength and potency and has often been regarded as a protective charm, with the Roman naturalist Pliny the Elder writing of its ability to ward off scorpions and snakes. The English herbalist Nicholas Culpeper assigned it to the planet Mars – with Mars being the God of War – writing that garlic's heat 'is very vehement'. In Chinese folklore, garlic is also seen as protective. It was, for example, traditionally eaten at the dragon boat festival (or Duanwu festival) to fend off evil spirits. Bulbs of garlic were even discovered in the tomb of King Tutankhamun, as the ancient Egyptians believed that it would protect them in the afterlife.

One feels that garlic's powerful, penetrating scent must have played a part in its mighty reputation; certainly in the most notorious of its properties –

the ability to protect against vampires. This is an association so famous that its legend lives on, even now in the twenty-first century garlic-laden dishes are jokingly said to 'keep the vampires away'. The tradition is particularly associated with Slavic folklore and famously with Transylvania. During the eighteenth century in Transylvania, fear of vampires was widespread, graves were dug up and bodies staked to prevent them returning in vampiric form and preying on people. Garlic, long seen as a charm with health-giving properties, especially among Transylvania's rural communities, was widely used as a protection – hung in or spread on doorways and window sills as a deterrent to form a barrier and so ensure the safety of those inside. Such was its reputed power that garlic cloves were placed in the mouths of the dead bodies of suspected vampires in order to weaken them and prevent them preying on the living. Reputedly, garlic was also used as a way of detecting vampires hidden in the community, with anyone refusing to eat a clove of garlic in church falling under suspicion. In his influential, much-filmed novel *Dracula*, the best-known of vampire stories, author Bram Stoker referred to this ancient custom, describing how the vampire hunter Van Helsing seeks to protect Lucy from the Count by giving her a necklace of garlic and spreading it on the entrances to her room. Vampires were not the only evils to be safeguarded against with garlic, it was also said to protect against the 'evil eye', demons, witches and werewolves.

Garlic's long-held – indeed still current – reputation as an aphrodisiac is thought to be linked to the suggestive shape of the spear-shaped plant and its bulbs. It is particularly striking just how many cultures around the world associate garlic with lust and love, as an ingredient that inflames passions. In traditional Indian Ayurvedic medicine, garlic is categorized as rajasic and tamasic, that is a food which promotes passion and ignorance. So, while in Ayurvedic medicine garlic is recommended as a tonic for loss of sexual power, it is shunned as a food by those seeking to reach a higher spiritual plane, therefore avoided by Buddhists, devout Hindus and Jains. In Greek mythology, garlic inflamed the romantic desires of King Minos and his wife Pasiphaë, who gave birth to the Minotaur. Aristotle, the Ancient Greek philosopher (384–322 BC) listed garlic as an aphrodisiac. In the writings of the Talmud, garlic is credited with encouraging love and healing the sick. In popular culture and consciousness, garlic's reputation as a plant with potent power endures; it is an interesting aspect of our abiding fascination with this special ingredient.

Fettunta

The original 'garlic bread', this Italian dish is traditionally made using the new season's olive oil, although any good-quality extra virgin olive oil can be used. In classic Italian fashion, simple ingredients combine to great effect. The name translates literally as 'oily slice', but it is far more delicious than this name may suggest. Although quick and simple to make, it is incredibly tasty. Try it!

4 thick slices of rustic bread
1 garlic clove, peeled
4 tablespoons extra virgin olive oil
salt (optional)

a griddle pan

Makes 4 slices

Preheat a griddle pan until hot. Griddle the bread for 2–3 minutes on each side until golden-brown and nicely striped. If you don't have a griddle pan, preheat a grill/broiler and toast until golden brown on each side.

Immediately rub one side of each slice with the garlic clove. Pour a tablespoon of olive oil over each slice. Add a pinch of salt, if using, and serve at once.

Roast garlic tartiflette

This classic French dish is a fine example of comfort food, with roast garlic adding a mellow richness to the indulgent layers of creamy sliced potatoes and melted cheese. Serve with a crisp green salad. Reblochon is the traditional cheese used in an authentic tartiflette, giving it a distinctive flavour and texture.

1 tablespoon vegetable oil

1 onion, halved and finely sliced

100 g/3½ oz. pancetta or bacon, cubed

300 ml/1¼ cups crème fraîche or sour cream

300 ml/1¼ cups whole milk

3 sprigs of fresh thyme, leaves picked

3 roast garlic cloves (see page 23), peeled and crushed to a paste

800 g/1¾ lbs. waxy potatoes, such as Charlottes, very finely sliced

½ Reblochon cheese, thinly sliced with rind left on

salt and freshly ground black pepper

1.5-litre/50-fl oz ovenproof dish, greased

Serves 4

Preheat oven to 200°C (400°F) Gas 6.

Heat the oil in a frying pan/skillet. Add the onion and fry, stirring often, until lightly browned and softened. Add the pancetta and fry, stirring, for 2–3 minutes.

In a large saucepan, mix together the crème fraîche, milk, thyme leaves and roast garlic paste. Season with salt and pepper. Bring to the boil and add the potato slices. Reduce the heat and simmer, covered, for 8 minutes. Mix in the fried pancetta and onion.

In a greased ovenproof dish, layer in a third of the crème fraîche and potato mixture. Top with a layer of Reblochon slices. Repeat the process, finishing with a layer of cheese.

Bake for 1 hour in the preheated oven until the potato slices are tender and the dish is golden brown.

Serve warm from the oven.

Spanish garlic soup

Garlic is at the heart of this rustic Spanish soup, sopa de ajo. The chicken stock is the key to its success, so if not making your own, buy the best quality stock you can find. Don't be tempted to use a stock cube!

2 tablespoons olive oil
4 garlic cloves, sliced
salt
1 teaspoon sweet Spanish
  paprika
4 slices of rustic bread
chopped fresh parsley,
  to garnish

CHICKEN STOCK
700 g/1½ lbs. chicken wings
1.2 litres/5 cups water

1 onion, chopped
1 carrot, chopped
2 celery stalks, chopped
1 garlic clove, peeled
5 peppercorns
(or 1 litre/4¼ cups good-
  quality chicken stock)
a handful of fresh parsley,
  to garnish

Serves 4

First make the stock. Place all the stock ingredients in a large pan. Bring to the boil, then cover, reduce the heat and simmer for 1 hour. Strain and reserve the chicken stock.

To make the soup, heat the olive oil in a large saucepan. Add the garlic and fry gently, stirring, until it turns pale gold. Take care not to burn it, as this would make it bitter. Add the stock and season with salt. Bring to the boil, then reduce the heat and simmer for 10–15 minutes, until heated through. Stir in the paprika.

Toast or grill/broil the bread. Place a slice in each of four soup bowls, pour over the soup, garnish with parsley and serve at once.

Roast garlic mac 'n' cheese

This is a luxurious take on traditional macaroni cheese, with the roast garlic adding a richness to the cheese sauce, elevating it from an everyday supper dish to something rather special. Serve with a crisp green salad.

200 g/1¾ cups macaroni or short penne pasta
1 teaspoon sunflower or vegetable oil
75 g/2¾ oz. pancetta or bacon, finely chopped
50 g/3½ tablespoons butter
50 g/6 tablespoons plain/all-purpose flour
600 ml/2½ cups whole milk
50 ml/3½ tablespoons double/heavy cream
125 g/1½ cups Cheddar cheese, grated

freshly grated nutmeg
3 roast garlic cloves (see page 23), peeled and crushed
75 g/½ cup cooked frozen peas
2 tablespoons grated Parmesan cheese
25 g/½ cup fresh breadcrumbs
salt and freshly ground black pepper

a shallow ovenproof dish, greased

Serves 4

Cook the macaroni in a large saucepan of salted boiling water until al dente; drain.

Meanwhile, heat the oil in a frying pan/skillet. Add the pancetta and fry, stirring often, until lightly browned and crisped.

Preheat the oven to 200°C (400°F) Gas 6.

Make the cheese sauce. Melt the butter in a heavy-based saucepan. Add the flour, whisking in well and cooking for 1 minute, stirring. Gradually add in the milk, stirring well with each addition to prevent any lumps forming. Bring to the boil, stirring, until thickened. Stir in the cream, then mix in the grated Cheddar cheese (reserving 2 tablespoons for the topping), stirring until melted. Season with salt, pepper and grated nutmeg. Mix in the roast garlic.

Mix together the macaroni, pancetta, peas and cheese sauce and transfer to the shallow ovenproof dish. Top with a layer of the remaining Cheddar, the Parmesan cheese and breadcrumbs.

Bake in the preheated oven for 20 minutes until golden brown on top, then serve at once.

Roast garlic fish pie

This luxurious version of a fish pie, with its creamy filling contrasting with the savoury mash, is perfect for dinner parties. Serve with the Italian-style Garlic Spinach (see page 31) as an accompaniment.

500 ml/2 cups good-quality fish stock

800 g/1¾ lbs. white fish fillet, skinned, cut into 4-cm/1½-in. chunks

1.5 kg/3¼ lbs. floury potatoes, such as King Edwards, peeled and chopped into chunks

a dash of milk

4½ tablespoons butter

3 roast garlic cloves (see page 23), peeled and mashed to a paste

freshly grated nutmeg

1 shallot, finely chopped

40 g/4¾ tablespoons plain/all-purpose flour

150 ml/⅔ cup double/ heavy cream

2 tablespoons finely chopped parsley

grated zest of ½ lemon

200 g/7 oz. cooked peeled prawns/shrimp

8 quail's eggs, hard-boiled/ hard-cooked, shelled and halved

25 g/¼ cup grated Cheddar cheese

salt and freshly ground black pepper

Serves 6

In a large saucepan, bring the fish stock to the boil. Add in the fish and simmer for 2–3 minutes until cooked through. Strain, reserving the stock, and set the fish aside to cool.

Make the roast garlic mash. Boil the potatoes in salted boiling water until tender; drain. Add the milk, 1 tablespoon of the butter and the roast garlic paste and mash together well. Season with pepper and nutmeg to taste.

Make the sauce. Heat the remaining butter in a heavy-based saucepan. Add the shallot and fry gently for 1–2 minutes until softened. Mix in the flour and cook, stirring, for 1 minute. Gradually add the fish stock, stirring to incorporate the flour well and ensure a lump-free sauce. Bring to the boil, stirring until it thickens. Stir in the cream, parsley and lemon zest. Set aside to cool.

Preheat the oven to 200°C (400°F) Gas 6.

Place the cooked fish, peeled prawns/shrimp and quail's eggs in a large ovenproof dish. Pour over the sauce and gently fold together. Spread over the garlic mash in an even layer. Sprinkle with the Cheddar cheese.

Bake for 30–40 minutes in the preheated oven until golden brown and piping hot. Serve at once.

Cider and garlic roast belly pork

A splendid and succulent slow-cooked pork dish, with the apple flavours of the cider cutting nicely through the richness of the pork. Stuffing prunes with mellow, smoky black garlic adds an extra tasty touch. This dish is great served with mashed potato and buttered cabbage.

2 kg/4½ lbs. belly pork on the bone, skin scored for crackling

6 garlic cloves, 4 left whole and 2 crushed

1 tablespoon finely chopped fresh thyme

2 large carrots, halved lengthways and chopped

1 onion, cut into chunks

500 ml/2¼ cups dry cider

300 ml/1¼ cups apple juice

8 pitted prunes

8 black garlic cloves

butter, for frying

salt and freshly ground black pepper

Serves 8

Bring the pork to room temperature and pat dry with paper towels. Preheat the oven to 220°C (425°F) Gas 7.

Season the flesh of the pork with salt and pepper, rubbing the salt generously into the scored skin. Mix together the crushed garlic and thyme into a paste. Rub the paste over the pork flesh.

Place the carrot, onion and whole garlic cloves in a roasting pan, then top with the seasoned pork belly so it rests on the vegetables. Pour the cider into the roasting pan.

Roast the pork for 30 minutes in the preheated oven then reduce the heat to 180°C (350°F) Gas 4 and roast for a further 2 hours, adding the apple juice to the roasting pan halfway through the cooking time.

Rest the pork in warm place. Blend the roast vegetables, garlic and cider mixture until smooth to form a gravy. Season with salt and pepper.

Fill each of the pitted prunes with a whole black garlic clove. Heat the butter in a small frying pan/skillet and fry the prunes briefly to heat through.

Serve the roast pork with the cider gravy and black garlic prunes.

Spanish-style garlic baked beans

My Spanish-inspired take on baked beans is a hearty, full-flavoured dish. Serve hot, warm or at room temperature with rustic bread to mop up the tasty sauce, and with a green salad on the side for contrast.

400 g/2½ cups borlotti/cranberry beans

1 tablespoon olive oil

1 onion, finely chopped

1 celery stalk, finely chopped

2 garlic cloves, chopped

1 tablespoon freshly chopped rosemary leaves

2 cooking chorizo (200–300 g/7–10 oz.), sliced

150 g/5½ oz. pancetta or bacon, diced

1 teaspoon sweet Spanish smoked paprika

400 ml/2 cups passata/strained tomatoes

salt and freshly ground black pepper

2 tablespoons freshly chopped parsley

a lidded flameproof casserole dish

Serves 6–8

Soak the beans in plenty of cold water overnight. Drain, place in a large pan and cover generously with cold water. Bring to the boil, reduce the heat and simmer for 45–60 minutes, until the beans are tender. Drain and set aside, reserving the cooking water.

Preheat the oven to 150°C (300°F) Gas 2.

Heat the olive oil in a flameproof casserole dish. Add the onion and celery and fry gently for 2 minutes, until softened. Add the garlic and rosemary, fry briefly until fragrant, then add the chorizo and pancetta. Fry, stirring often, for 3–5 minutes. Sprinkle over the paprika, and stir in the passata/strained tomatoes and 400 ml/1¾ cups of the reserved bean water (keep the remaining bean water to top up). Season with salt. Add the beans.

Bring to the boil, cover and transfer to the preheated oven to bake for 2 hours, checking now and then whether the beans are drying out during this stage and adding more bean water if necessary.

Transfer the dish from the oven to the stovetop, uncover and simmer gently for 30 minutes, stirring now and then, to reduce and thicken the sauce. Taste and season with salt and pepper as required. Garnish with parsley and serve at once.

Italian sausages with garlic lentils

Sausages and lentils make the perfect partners. This is an easy, filling meal full of robust flavours — comfort food Italian style! If possible, use fresh Italian pork sausages, which are often flavoured with garlic and fennel, as their texture and taste work well with the lentils.

400 g/2 cups Castelluccio
    or Puy lentils, rinsed
1 carrot, finely diced
300 ml/1¼ cups red wine
1 litre/4¼ cups cold water
3 garlic cloves, peeled and
    left whole
1 fresh bay leaf
3 fresh sage leaves
½ tablespoon vegetable oil
8 Italian sausages (or good-
    quality meaty sausages)
3 tablespoons extra virgin
    olive oil
4 tablespoons freshly
    chopped parsley
salt

Serves 4

Preheat the oven to 200°C (400°F) Gas 6. Place a roasting pan in the oven to preheat.

Place the rinsed lentils and diced carrot in a large saucepan. Add the red wine, water, garlic, bay leaf and sage. Bring to the boil, then reduce the heat and simmer for 20–25 minutes until the lentils are tender but retain some texture. Add salt to the lentils to season, then drain.

While the lentils are cooking, heat the vegetable oil in a large frying pan/skillet. Add the sausages and brown quickly on all sides. Transfer the browned sausages to the preheated roasting pan and bake in the oven for 20–25 minutes until cooked through.

Pick out and discard the bay leaf and sage leaves from the lentils. Mash the garlic cloves. Toss the cooked lentils with the mashed garlic, olive oil and parsley. Top with the sausages and serve at once.

Boeuf bourguignon

This classic French dish is a rich combination of slow-cooked, tender, wine-marinated beef, flavoured with herbs, bacon, mushrooms and garlic. Serve it with creamy mashed potatoes and green beans. As it can be made in advance, this is an ideal dish for entertaining.

800 g/1¾ lbs. braising steak, cubed

750 ml/3¼ cups red wine, ideally Burgundy

1 onion, roughly chopped

1 carrot, roughly chopped

3 garlic cloves, chopped

4 fresh thyme sprigs

2 fresh bay leaves

2 tablespoons olive oil

1 shallot, chopped

2 rashers/slices smoked bacon, chopped into fine strips

400 ml/1¾ cups beef stock

15 g/1 tablespoon butter

200 g/7 oz. button mushrooms

salt and freshly ground black pepper

chopped parsley, to serve

a lidded flameproof casserole dish

Serves 6 – 8

Place the steak in a large bowl with the red wine, onion, carrot, garlic, thyme and bay leaves and marinate in the fridge for at least 3 hours, or ideally overnight.

Preheat the oven to 150°C (300°F) Gas 2.

Remove the beef from the marinade and pat dry with kitchen paper. Discard the onion and carrot, but reserve the rest of the red wine marinade (i.e. the wine, garlic and herbs). Place the reserved red wine marinade in a pan, bring to the boil and cook uncovered until reduced to about 600 ml/2½ cups.

Heat 1 tablespoon olive oil in a casserole dish. Add the beef and fry for 3–5 minutes until browned on all sides. Set aside.

Wipe out the casserole dish with paper towels. Add the remaining olive oil, heat through and fry the shallot and bacon for 1–2 minutes, until fragrant. Add the browned beef, reduced red wine and the beef stock. Season with salt and pepper. Bring to the boil, cover and cook in the preheated oven for 2 hours.

Towards the end of the casserole's cooking time, heat the butter in a frying pan/skillet and fry the mushrooms until golden brown. Stir the mushrooms into the casserole and serve garnished with chopped parsley.

Garlic butter roast chicken

Roast chicken is an all-time favourite and always makes a great family meal. Adding the butter under the skin results in a moist, tasty chicken, aromatic from herbs and garlic. Serve with Garlicky Goose Fat Roast Potatoes (see page 31) or Garlic and Almond Purple Sprouting Broccoli (see page 60).

3 garlic cloves, 2 peeled and 1 unpeeled

70 g/5 tablespoons butter, softened

2 tablespoons finely chopped fresh parsley

1 teaspoon lemon thyme leaves or thyme leaves

grated zest and freshly squeezed juice of ½ lemon (save the lemon half after squeezing as it will be used in the recipe)

1 oven-ready chicken, approx. 2 kg/4½ lbs.

salt and freshly ground black pepper

GRAVY

½ tablespoon olive oil

½ onion, finely chopped

1 fresh bay leaf

splash of white wine

300 ml/1¼ cups chicken stock

Serves 4

Preheat the oven to 200°C (400°F) Gas 6.

Make the garlic butter by pounding the peeled garlic into a paste with a pinch of salt. Mix together 50 g/3½ tablespoons of the butter with the garlic paste, parsley, lemon thyme and lemon zest.

Season the chicken with salt and pepper. Place on a rack in a roasting pan. Place the unpeeled garlic clove and the squeezed lemon half inside the chicken cavity. Pour over the lemon juice.

Using your fingers, gently pull the skin away from the chicken breast. Insert the garlic butter under the skin and on to the flesh, pressing down to spread it evenly over the chicken breast. Dot the remaining butter over the chicken legs and wings.

Roast the chicken in the preheated oven for 1 hour 20 minutes – 1 hour 30 minutes, basting often with butter juices, until cooked through and the juices run clear. Rest for 15 minutes.

Meanwhile, use the roasting juices to make a gravy. Skim off excess fat from the roasting juices. Heat the oil in a pan, add the onion and bay leaf and fry gently until the onion has softened. Add the wine, cook briefly, then add the stock and the roasting juices. Bring to the boil and cook until slightly reduced. Season as required. Discard the bay leaf and serve at once with the chicken.

Fiery garlic

Meet the garlic farmers

South West Garlic Farm, Dorset, England

Farmer Mark Botwright's interest in growing food dates back to his days as a boy, when he looked after the family's vegetable plot. His fascination with garlic, however, dates back to a birthday present of elephant garlic from his wife. Mark planted them in his garden, grew them, dried them and replanted the cloves, growing his garlic collection until he had thousands of bulbs and a range of varieties.

Such was his obsession that Mark decided to switch from sheep farming to garlic farming and has now established a flourishing business on his Dorset-based South West Garlic Farm, growing Iberian, Morado, Violet Spring and (naturally) elephant garlic. His customers include top British restaurants and high-end food stores, attracted by both the provenance and the exceptional quality of his fresh produce.

Mark's genuine interest in ingredients and cooking, together with an adventurous willingness to innovate, have fed into his business. The cult popularity among chefs of garlic scapes – the edible stalks of garlic (which had been previously discarded by garlic growers in the UK) – is something he has pioneered. He also offers black garlic, created by gently heating

garlic bulbs for 40–50 days until the cloves darken and soften, taking on a distinctive sweet-sourness.

Filaree Garlic Farm, Omak, Washington, USA

Filaree was founded in 1977 by Ron Engeland, initially as an heirloom apple orchard. During the mid 1980s, however, Ron began growing garlic in between the trees. His fascination with heritage varieties saw him contacting university researchers in a quest for unusual garlic varieties, and the farm at one stage grew a staggering 300 varieties.

Today, this organic farm grows over 100 varieties of garlic and supplies seed garlic to other growers. Now owned by Alley Swiss, Filaree is North America's largest privately owned collection of garlic, deeply committed to its self-proclaimed mission to preserve and promote its diverse range of unique garlic varieties, many of which trace their origins to Germany's Gatersleben seed bank. Growing so many varieties of garlic allows for the diversity of garlic to be revealed and appreciated. Among the strains cultivated by Filaree are hot-flavoured, purple-striped Turban strains, large-cloved Porcelain strains, rich-tasting Rocambole and sweet Creole.

The farm's location in an arid desert region means that they are free from many of the hazardous pests and diseases normally associated with garlic. The crop is lovingly tended, with the weeding done by hand, irrigation from mountain-fed spring water, the fields regularly walked to check the health of the plants and much of the garlic selectively harvested at the peak of its maturity.

La Maison de l'Ail, Saint-Clar, France

France has a venerable tradition of protecting its historic foodstuffs and garlic is among the ingredients recognized in this way. It has long been cultivated in the department of Lomagne in south-west France, thriving in its favourable climate and ideal clay and

limestone soils, and becoming an important crop in the area. Since 2004, Lomagne white garlic has been granted Indication Géographique Protégée (IGP) status. Around 300 growers in the region grow this highly regarded white garlic, used in local dishes such as *tourin*, a simple, rustic garlic soup.

Among them are farmers Monsieur and Madame Gamot who, in 2000, founded La Maison de l'Ail in an old barn on their farm to celebrate the region's garlic. Exhibitions, sculptures and festive events such as a market and an annual garlic competition, attended by local garlic farmers, offer a chance to learn about garlic and how it is cultivated in the region.

The Gamots are firm believers in the healthy virtues of garlic, both for humans and for the soil. On their farm they grow white garlic, planted in the autumn, then harvested on the Feast of St John on June 24th, and also violet garlic, harvested in late summer. The garlic is picked, dried for a month, plaited and sold from July through to October.

Piquant peanut and garlic relish

Peanut butter lovers will appreciate this savoury, nutty, chilli/chile-piquant relish.
It makes an excellent accompaniment to grilled meats or fish.

**25 g/1 cup freshly chopped
  parsley stalks and leaves**

**2 heaped tablespoons
  peanut butter**

1 tomato

1 red chilli/chile, chopped

2 garlic cloves, chopped

**2-cm/3/4-in. fresh ginger,
  peeled and chopped**

**1 tablespoon groundnut or
  sunflower oil**

Makes about
220 g/8 oz.

Place all the ingredients in a food processor and blend into a paste.
Cover and chill to store, but serve at room temperature.

This relish is best eaten fresh when the flavours are strongest.
However, any leftovers can be stored in the fridge, covered with
a thin layer of oil to prevent discolouring, for up to 2 days.

Herb and garlic chutney

Tangy with a kick of chilli/chile, this fresh chutney has an exuberant zing to it. Serve as a relish alongside Indian dishes such as tandoori chicken.

100 g/2 cups fresh coriander/cilantro, stalks and leaves
2 garlic cloves, chopped
50 g/⅓ cup blanched almonds
1 teaspoon cumin seeds, toasted and finely ground
1 green chilli/chile, chopped
freshly squeezed juice of 1–2 lemons
1 teaspoon salt
1 teaspoon sugar

Makes about 220 g/8 oz.

Rinse the coriander/cilantro well, discarding any wilted leaves, and chop. In a food processor, blitz together the coriander/cilantro, garlic, almonds, cumin and chilli/chile to a paste. Gradually add in the lemon juice, salt and sugar, blitzing to mix well and tasting to ensure a balance of sweetness, sourness and saltiness.

Cover and chill until serving. This chutney is best eaten fresh when the flavours are at their strongest. However, any leftovers can be stored in the fridge for up to 2 days. Cover with a thin layer of oil to prevent discolouring.

Smoky garlic baba ghanoush

This Middle Eastern–inspired dip has a pleasant, subtly smoky garlic flavour. Roasting aubergines/eggplant until the skin is charred softens the flesh and mellows their flavour. Serve it with warm pitta bread and crudités as a vegetarian appetizer, or with other dishes, such as Hummus (see page 14) or Tzatziki (see page 55) as part of a mezze meal.

2 aubergines/eggplants
2 smoked garlic cloves
freshly squeezed juice of ½ lemon
3 tablespoons extra virgin olive oil, plus extra to serve
salt

TO GARNISH
1 tablespoon natural yogurt
a pinch of ground sumac
freshly chopped parsley

a foil-lined baking sheet

Makes about 400 g/14 oz.

Preheat the oven to 200°C (400°F) Gas 6.

Place the aubergines/eggplants on a foil-lined baking sheet and roast in the preheated oven for 1 hour, turning over halfway through, until charred on all sides. Place the hot aubergines/eggplants in a plastic bag (so that the resulting steam will make the skin easier to peel off) and set aside to cool.

Peel the roasted aubergines/eggplants and chop the flesh into chunks. Crush the smoked garlic with a pinch of salt into a paste. In a food processor, blend together the roast aubergines/eggplants, smoked garlic paste, lemon juice and olive oil into a smooth purée. Season with salt.

Place in a serving bowl and spoon over the yogurt. Top with sumac, a little olive oil, add parsley and serve.

Kimchi pancake with black garlic crème fraîche

My take on this popular Korean dish contrasts the chewy-textured, chilli/chile-hot pancake with the subtle coolness of crème fraîche, enriched with the mellow sweetness of black garlic. Kimchi is a traditional Korean fermented relish, usually made with cabbage.

100 g/¾ cup plain/all-purpose flour

½ teaspoon salt

100 ml/⅓ cup water

3 tablespoons kimchi liquid (reserved from kimchi)

130 g/1 cup kimchi, finely chopped

1 spring onion/scallion, finely chopped

150 ml/⅔ cup crème fraîche or sour cream

3 black garlic cloves, finely chopped

1 tablespoon sunflower or vegetable oil

thinly sliced spring onion/scallion, to garnish

Serves 4 as an appetizer or 2 as a main course

Make the batter by whisking together the flour, salt and water into a thick paste. Stir in the kimchi liquid, then mix in the kimchi and spring onion/scallion.

Mix together the crème fraîche and black garlic and set aside.

Heat a large frying pan/skillet until hot. Add the oil and heat well. Pour in the batter, which should sizzle as it hits the pan, spreading it to form an even layer. Fry for 3–5 minutes until set, then turn over and fry the pancake for a further 3–4 minutes until it is well browned on both sides.

Cut the kimchi pancake into portions and serve topped with the black garlic crème fraîche. Sprinkle with extra spring onions/scallions to garnish.

Spaghetti con aglio, olio e peperoncino

So simple but so good, this homely pasta dish of garlic, oil and chilli/chile is an Italian classic. Made in minutes using store-cupboard staples, it's a great speedy meal. A generous quantity of garlic is traditional as it is the dish's key flavouring.

450 g/1 lb. spaghetti
150 ml/²⁄₃ cup extra virgin olive oil
8 garlic cloves, finely chopped
6 pepperoncini (small Italian dried chilli/chile peppers), chopped
6 tablespoons finely chopped fresh parsley
salt and freshly ground black pepper
grated Parmesan cheese, to serve

Serves 4

Cook the spaghetti in a large pan of salted, boiling water until it becomes al dente.

Meanwhile, heat the olive oil in a small, heavy-based frying pan/skillet. Add the garlic and pepperoncini and fry gently over a low heat, stirring often, until the garlic turns golden brown. Take care not to burn the garlic as this would make it bitter. Set the garlic pepperoncini oil aside to infuse.

Once the spaghetti is cooked, drain well and return to the saucepan. Gently reheat the oil and pour over the spaghetti, mixing well. Sprinkle with parsley and serve at once with Parmesan cheese.

Malay garlic and chilli/chile prawns/shrimp

A quickly cooked, piquant king prawn/jumbo shrimp dish, fragrant with lemongrass and kaffir lime leaves. Serve with coconut rice as a soothing contrast.

2 lemongrass stalks

150 g/1 cup tomatoes, chopped

1 onion, chopped

2 garlic cloves, chopped

2 tablespoons tomato purée/paste

1 red chilli/chile, de-seeded and chopped

a pinch of sugar

2 tablespoons sunflower or vegetable oil

2 kaffir lime leaves, central vein discarded, finely shredded

300 g/10½ oz. raw king prawns/jumbo shrimp, peeled and deveined

salt

finely chopped spring onion/scallion, to garnish

Serves 4

First make a paste. Remove the tough outer casing from the lemongrass stalks and finely chop the white, bulbous part, discarding the rest. In a food processor, blend together the lemongrass, tomatoes, onion, garlic, tomato purée/paste, chilli/chile and sugar, set aside.

Heat a wok until hot. Add the oil and heat through. Add the shredded kaffir lime leaves and blended paste and fry, stirring often, for 7–8 minutes until cooked through and reduced.

Add the prawns/shrimp, season with salt, and stir-fry, until the prawns/shrimp turn opaque and are cooked through – this takes just a few minutes. Serve at once, garnished with the finely chopped spring onion/scallion.

Thai-style fish with fried garlic

This recipe is a great way of cooking a fish fillet, with the crisp garlic flakes adding both flavour and texture. Serve with rice and a green vegetable, such as spinach or pak choi/bok choy.

1 lemongrass stalk
500 g/1 lb. 2 oz. white fish fillet (such as cod)
2 tablespoons sunflower or vegetable oil
1½ tablespoons fish sauce
1 shallot, finely chopped
1 red chilli/chile, de-seeded and finely chopped
4 garlic cloves, sliced finely lengthways
freshly ground black pepper

Serves 4

Preheat the oven to 200°C (400°F) Gas 6.

Remove the tough outer casing from the lemongrass. Finely chop the white, bulbous part, discarding the rest.

Place the fish skin side-down in a shallow ovenproof dish or roasting pan. Mix together 1 tablespoon of the oil, the fish sauce, shallot, chilli/chile and lemongrass, season with pepper and pour evenly over the fish, coating it well. Bake the fish for 15–20 minutes until cooked through.

Just before the fish has finished cooking, heat the remaining oil in a small frying pan/skillet. Add the garlic and fry until golden-brown, taking care not to burn it, as this would make it bitter. Pour the hot garlic and oil over the cooked fish and serve at once.

Garlic chive meatballs

500 g/1 lb. 2 oz. ground pork
25 g/1 oz. Chinese or garlic
  chives, finely chopped
1 garlic clove, finely chopped
1 cm/½ in. fresh ginger,
  peeled and finely chopped
1 egg white
1 tablespoon light soy sauce
1 teaspoon salt
½ teaspoon ground white
  or black pepper
1 teaspoon sesame oil
2 teaspoons cornflour/
  cornstarch

DIPPING SAUCE
3 tablespoons light soy sauce
1 teaspoon sesame oil
½ red chilli/chile, de-seeded
  and finely chopped

a steamer

Serves 4

This is a simple, homely dish. Steaming the meatballs, rather than frying them, is an easy and healthy way of cooking them. Serve with rice or noodles and Chinese greens such as pak choi/bok choy or gai lan (also known as Chinese broccoli or Chinese kale).

Blend all the meatball ingredients together in a food processor until thoroughly mixed. With wet hands to prevent sticking, shape the mixture into small meatballs, each the size of a large marble.

Steam the meatballs for 20 minutes until cooked through.

Mix together the dipping sauce ingredients. Serve the meatballs with the dipping sauce.

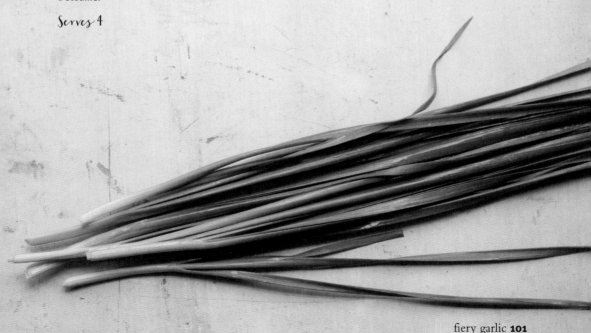

Thai-style fried garlic minced/ground chicken

A truly tasty dish, inspired by Thai flavours. Serve with steamed rice for a simple, yet satisfying meal, ideal for a midweek supper. If green beans are not available, tenderstem broccoli would make a good substitute.

2 tablespoons sunflower or vegetable oil
2 garlic cloves, finely chopped
1 shallot, finely sliced
100 g/3½ oz. green beans, topped, tailed and cut into 1-cm/³⁄₈-in. pieces
4 button mushrooms, chopped
400 g/14 oz. minced/ground chicken
1 red chilli/chile, de-seeded, finely chopped (optional)
1 teaspoon dark brown sugar
1 tablespoon fish sauce
1 tablespoon dark soy sauce
3 tablespoons chicken stock
freshly ground black pepper
Thai basil or basil leaves, to garnish

Serves 4

Heat a wok until hot. Add the oil and heat through. Add the garlic and shallot and fry, stirring, until garlic turns pale gold. Add the green beans and fry, stirring, for 1 minute. Add the mushrooms and fry, stirring, for 1 minute.

Add the minced/ground chicken and fry, stirring with a spatula to break up any lumps, until lightened on all sides. Add the chilli/chile, if using, and mix in well. Add the sugar, fish sauce and soy sauce and mix in. Add the stock and stir-fry for 5 minutes until the stock has cooked off and the ingredients are well mixed.

Season generously with black pepper, garnish with basil leaves and serve at once.

400 g/14 oz. rump steak,
finely sliced into short
strips

MARINADE
2 tablespoons sesame seeds,
dry-fried until golden
brown
3 garlic cloves, crushed
with pinch of salt to make
a paste
1 teaspoon sugar
3 spring onions/scallions,
sliced into 2-cm/
¾-in. lengths
4 tablespoons light soy
sauce
2 tablespoons sesame oil
2.5-cm/1-in. fresh ginger,
peeled and finely chopped

DIPPING SAUCE
3 tablespoons light soy sauce
1 tablespoon sesame oil
1 tablespoon rice wine or
medium sherry
1 teaspoon Korean soy bean
paste
1 tablespoon sesame seeds,
dry-fried until golden
brown
1 spring onion/scallion,
finely chopped
1 garlic clove, finely chopped
1 teaspoon sugar
½ teaspoon dried chilli
flakes/hot pepper flakes

Serves 4

Bulgogi

This famous Korean dish, consisting of savoury,
tender beef strips, is addictively good. Make sure you
allow sufficient time for marinating, as this is essential
for locking the flavours in. Serve with rice or noodles
and Chinese greens on the side.

Mix together the marinade ingredients. Add the steak strips and
toss to coat thoroughly. Cover and marinate in the fridge for at least
6 hours, ideally overnight.

Mix together the dipping sauce ingredients and set aside.

Bring the marinated beef out of the fridge 30 minutes before
cooking, to allow it to come to room temperature.

Preheat a large, heavy-based frying pan/skillet or griddle pan until
very hot. Add the beef strips in one layer to the pan. Cook briefly on
one side, then turn over to cook the other side, until browned on
both sides – this takes just a few minutes in total.

Serve the beef at once with the dipping sauce.

Spicy Indian garlic meatballs

Minced/ground beef doesn't have to be dull, as this recipe proves with its array of spices. Serve these little meatballs with basmati rice and a vegetable side dish.

500 g/1 lb. 2 oz.
   minced/ground beef
1 garlic clove, crushed with
   a pinch of salt
1 teaspoon ground cumin
2 teaspoons ground
   coriander
2 tablespoons sunflower
   or vegetable oil
1 onion, finely chopped
1 garlic clove, chopped
2-cm/¾-in. fresh ginger,
   peeled and finely chopped
1 cinnamon stick
4 cardamom pods
handful of fresh or frozen
   (not dried) curry leaves
   (optional)
400-g/14-oz. can of chopped
   tomatoes
¼ teaspoon ground turmeric
¼ teaspoon chilli powder/
   hot red pepper powder
   (optional)
300 ml/1¼ cups water
salt and freshly ground black
   pepper
torn fresh coriander/cilantro
   leaves, to garnish

*a large lidded frying
   pan/skillet*

Serves 4

First, make the meatballs. Mix together the beef, crushed garlic, cumin and coriander and season well with salt and pepper. With wet hands to prevent sticking, shape the mixture into small meatballs, each roughly the size of a large marble.

Heat 1 tablespoon of the oil in a large, lidded frying pan/skillet and fry the meatballs until browned on all sides. Set aside.

Add the remaining oil to the pan. Fry the onion, chopped garlic clove, ginger, cinnamon stick and cardamom pods, stirring, until the onion has softened. Mix in the curry leaves, if using, frying briefly, then add the chopped tomatoes. Add in the turmeric, chilli/hot red pepper powder and water. Season with salt. Bring to the boil.

Add the browned meatballs, bring to the boil once more, then cover, reduce the heat and cook for 15 minutes, stirring now and then. Uncover and cook for 10 further minutes, stirring often, until the sauce has reduced and thickened. Serve at once, garnished with fresh coriander/cilantro.

Go wild garlic

Growing garlic

One of the reasons for garlic's universal popularity is the plant's ability to thrive in a range of climates and soils. Just as it is versatile in the kitchen, so garlic is adaptable as a plant, growing in both cold northern climates and in tropical countries. While garlic grows well in the ground, it does not require a lot of space and can also be grown successfully in pots, making it an excellent addition to a potted herb collection.

Choosing your garlic

Garlic is grown from individual cloves. While it is possible to simply plant garlic cloves bought from a food shop, because of the risk of disease it is recommended that you source your seed garlic from a plant nursery or grower.

Bear in mind that the larger the clove, the larger the plant will be, so choose the biggest cloves, keeping on their papery husk. Separate cloves from the bulb just before planting, rather than in advance.

There are several varieties of garlic to choose from, with variations including white and violet-coloured bulbs and flavour ranging from mild and sweet to hot and fiery. Garlic (*Allium sativum*) has two subspecies: softneck (*Allium sativum sativum*) and hardneck (*Allium sativum ophioscorodon*). Unlike softnecks, hardnecks produce a straight, central edible stalk. Traditionally, in order to produce larger bulbs, these stalks were cut; they are known as scapes.

When to plant

In cold climates, garlic is usually planted before the winter, to give the plants a chance to establish their root systems before the arrival of frosts. Spring planting, depending on the climate and variety, is

also possible. Plant the cloves root-end down about 5 cm/2 in. deep in soil, spaced 15 cm/6 in. apart if planting in a row. Garlic enjoys well-drained, rich soil but can grow in a variety of soils. The plants can be smothered easily by weeds, so be sure to weed the soil around them thoroughly.

As softneck garlic grows, it sends up green leaves, with hardnecks also sending up a straight stalk. Water garlic evenly, taking care not to overwater. When the leaves have grown, the plant will set its bulb. Once the bulb is established, the advice is not to water the garlic otherwise you risk rotting the bulb.

Harvesting

Garlic is harvested in the summer months, between June and August depending on the variety. When the leaves turn yellow, this is a sign that the bulb is ready to harvest. Many growers harvest when the lower leaves have turned yellow but the ones above are still green. Harvesting too early risks an underdeveloped bulb, while harvesting too late can result in a looser bulb, which won't store as well. To harvest, carefully loosen the soil around the plant, making sure you do not damage the bulb, and gently lift out the bulb by hand so as not to damage it.

Once the garlic has been lifted from the soil it needs to be dried or cured. Remove clumps of soil from the roots, but leave the roots on the bulb. Spread or hang the garlic in a cool, dry place, with good air circulation; hanging the garlic is ideal as this allows it to dry out evenly. Leave the garlic in these conditions for two weeks, so that the outer layer has dried but the garlic retains its moisture, then trim the roots and remove any dirty outer layers. Your garlic is ready to use.

Wild garlic/ramps hazelnut pesto

Wild garlic (or ramps) combined with hazelnuts gives this simple-to-make pesto a wonderfully distinctive flavour. Stir it into Pasta Primavera (page 120), spread it over chicken or fish before baking or use it as a tasty garnish for soups, such as sweet potato or carrot.

80 g/⅔ cup hazelnuts
80 g/3 oz. wild garlic leaves/
  ramps, thoroughly rinsed,
  roughly chopped
150 ml/⅔ cup extra virgin olive
  oil

50 g/⅔ cup grated Parmesan
  cheese
salt

*Makes about
350 g/12 oz.*

Dry-fry the hazelnuts in a heavy-based frying pan/skillet over a medium heat, stirring frequently, until golden brown. Set aside to cool, then finely grind.

If using a food processor, blitz the wild garlic/ramps into a paste. Add the ground hazelnuts and olive oil and briefly whizz together. Mix in the Parmesan cheese, then season with salt, bearing in mind the saltiness of the cheese.

If using a pestle and mortar, pound the wild garlic/ramps into a paste. Add in the ground hazelnuts and olive oil and pound to mix together. Mix in the Parmesan cheese, then season with salt.

If any of the pesto is left over, it can be stored in the fridge for up to 2 days; covering the surface with a thin layer of oil helps to preserve it. Alternatively, it can be frozen.

Wild garlic/ramps dough balls

Enjoy these truly tasty, savoury bread rolls freshly baked and warm from the oven. Serve them with soup for a first course or a light meal.

500 g/3½ cups strong bread flour, plus extra for dusting

1 teaspoon fast-action dried yeast

1½ teaspoons salt

1½ teaspoons sugar

300 ml/1¼ cups hand-hot water

2 tablespoons olive oil, plus extra for greasing

75 g/⅓ cup butter, softened

25 g/1 oz. wild garlic leaves/ ramps, rinsed well and finely chopped

2 baking sheets, lightly greased

Makes 24

First, make the bread dough. In a mixing bowl, mix together the flour, yeast, salt and sugar. Gradually add the hand-hot water and olive oil, bringing the mixture together to form a sticky dough. Turn out onto a lightly floured surface and knead well until the dough is smooth and elastic. Place in a clean, oiled mixing bowl, cover with a damp, clean kitchen cloth and set aside in a warm place to rise for 1 hour, during which time it should rise noticeably and almost double in size.

While the dough is rising, mix together the butter and wild garlic/ ramps thoroughly.

Preheat the oven to 220°C (425°F) Gas 7.

Gently heat the wild garlic butter in a pan until just melted.

Break down the risen dough and divide it into 24 even-sized portions, shaping each into a rounded ball shape. Place the dough balls on the greased baking sheets, spaced well apart. Brush each dough ball generously with the melted wild garlic/ramps butter.

Bake the dough balls for 15–20 minutes in the preheated oven until golden brown. Brush the freshly baked dough balls with the remaining wild garlic/ramps butter and serve at once.

Wild garlic/ramps goat's cheese flan

This stylish savoury tart, combining subtle goat's cheese with earthy wild garlic, has a delicate, moist texture. Serve with a crisp-textured salad for a light meal.

300 g/10½ oz. shortcrust pastry/pie dough

2 eggs plus 1 egg yolk

300 ml/1¼ cups crème fraîche or sour cream

25 g/1 oz. wild garlic leaves/ramps, thoroughly rinsed, finely chopped

freshly grated nutmeg

200 g/7 oz. white rind goat's cheese, sliced

salt and freshly ground black pepper

24-cm/9½-in. loose-based flan tin/quiche pan, lightly greased

Serves 6

Preheat the oven to 200°C (400°F) Gas 6.

First make the pastry case. Roll out the pastry/pie dough on a lightly floured work surface, then line the greased flan tin/quiche pan. Press it in firmly and prick the base several times to stop the pastry bubbling up. Line the case with a piece of parchment paper and fill with baking beans. Blind bake the pastry case for 15 minutes. Carefully remove the baking beans and paper and bake for a further 5 minutes.

While the pastry is baking, lightly whisk together the eggs, egg yolk and crème fraîche. Stir in the wild garlic/ramps and season with grated nutmeg, salt and pepper.

Layer the goat's cheese slices in the pastry case. Pour over the egg mixture. Bake for 40 minutes until risen and golden-brown. Serve warm or at room temperature.

Wild garlic/ramps cheese scones

Freshly baked scones, served warm from the oven and spread generously with butter, are always hard to resist. These savoury scones, with their earthy flavour, are no exception.

250 g/1¾ cups self-raising/self-rising flour

1 teaspoon baking powder

a pinch of salt

50 g/3½ tablespoons butter, diced, plus extra to serve

75 g/1 cup finely grated Cheddar cheese

1 egg

125 ml/½ cup buttermilk (or 100 ml/⅓ cup whole milk with 25 ml/2 tablespoons yogurt mixed in), plus extra for glazing

25 g/1 oz. wild garlic leaves/ramps, thoroughly rinsed and finely chopped

6-cm/2-in. cookie cutter

a baking sheet, greased

Makes 8

Preheat the oven to 220°C (425°F) Gas 7.

Sift the flour and baking powder into a mixing bowl. Mix in the salt. Rub in the butter with your fingertips until absorbed, then mix in the grated Cheddar.

Whisk the egg into the buttermilk. Pour the egg mixture into the flour mixture, add in the chopped wild garlic/ramps and mix together to form a soft, sticky dough.

Roll out the dough on a lightly floured work surface to a thickness of 2.5 cm/1 in. and use the cookie cutter to cut out the scones, reshaping and re-rolling the trimmings, to form 8 scones.

Place the scones on the greased baking sheet. Brush lightly with buttermilk.

Bake the scones for 10–15 minutes in the preheated oven until they have risen and are golden brown. Serve at once, split in half and spread with lashings of butter.

Wild garlic/ramps pasta primavera

Primavera means 'spring' in Italian and this simple yet elegant recipe makes use of seasonal ingredients to create a lovely fresh and light garlicky pasta dish.

1 tablespoon pine nuts
100 g/1 cup fresh asparagus, sliced into 2.5-cm/1-in. lengths
75 g/½ cup fresh peas (or frozen if preferred)
75 g/⅔ cup green/French beans, topped, tailed and sliced into short lengths
200 g/3 cups farfalle pasta

100 g/½ cup Wild Garlic/ Ramps Hazelnut Pesto (see page 112)
2 heaped tablespoons mascarpone cheese
grated Parmesan cheese, to serve

Serves 4

Put the pine nuts in a dry heavy-based frying pan/skillet set over a medium heat and toast, stirring often, until golden brown. Remove the pan from the heat and set aside.

Cook the asparagus, peas and green/French beans in separate pans of boiling water until just tender – you want them al dente. Drain at once, immerse in cold water to stop the cooking process, then drain again thoroughly.

Bring a large pan of salted water to the boil. Add the pasta and cook until al dente; drain.

Toss the freshly drained pasta first with the wild garlic/ramps pesto, then the mascarpone cheese, coating well. Add the asparagus, peas and green/French beans and toss together thoroughly. Scatter over the toasted pine nuts and serve at once, with Parmesan cheese sprinkled over the top.

Grilled wild garlic/ramps mussels

A rich, tasty way to serve mussels, this offers a great contrast of textures between the crunchy crumb crust and the juicy mussel flesh below.

1 kg/2¼ lbs. mussels
30 g/⅓ cup fresh breadcrumbs
15 g/¼ cup wild garlic leaves/ramps, thoroughly rinsed and very finely chopped
60 ml/¼ cup extra virgin olive oil
salt and freshly ground black pepper

Serves 4 as an appetizer or 2 as a main

Rinse the mussels well under cold running water, discarding any which are open or cracked. Scrub well to remove any beards or grit.

Put the cleaned mussels in a large pan, adding cold water to a depth of 2.5 cm/1 in. up the side of the pan. Set the pan over a medium heat, cover and cook the mussels for around 5 minutes, until they have steamed open.

Drain the mussels, discarding any that haven't opened during the cooking process.

Once the mussels are cool enough to handle, pull one half of each shell off each mussel, leaving the mussel anchored in the remaining half. Place the mussels, shell-side-down, on a baking sheet.

Mix together the breadcrumbs, wild garlic/ramps and olive oil, seasoning with salt and freshly ground pepper. Spoon a little of the breadcrumb mixture over each mussel, so that it forms a topping.

Preheat a grill/broiler to its highest setting and cook the topped mussels for 2–3 minutes until the crumb topping turns golden brown. Serve at once.

Wild garlic/ramps salmon en papillote

Cooking fish en papillote, that is 'wrapped in a parcel', is a great way of retaining both flavour and moisture. This recipe is for salmon, but other fillets of fish, such as sea bass, would also work well. Serve the salmon with new or mashed potatoes and green beans as an elegant dinner party dish.

40 g/3 tablespoons butter, softened
10 g/½ oz. wild garlic leaves/ramps, finely chopped
grated zest of 1 lemon
4 salmon fillets (each around 175 g/6 oz.)
2 tablespoons dry white wine
salt and freshly ground black pepper

4 squares of parchment paper, 30 x 30 cm/ 12 x 12 in.

Serves 4

Preheat the oven to 220°C (425°F) Gas 7.

Mix together the butter, wild garlic/ramps and lemon zest.

Fold each piece of baking parchment in half. Place each salmon fillet, skin-side-down, on one side of the crease in the paper. Season each fillet with salt and pepper, spread with a quarter of the wild garlic/ramps butter and spoon over a quarter of the wine. Fold the paper over the fillets and crimp the edges together, folding tightly.

Place the parcels on a baking sheet and bake for 15 minutes until puffed up. Serve at once, opening each parcel at the table.

Beef ale stew with wild garlic/ramps dumplings

A traditional dish of stew and suet dumplings, perfect for a hearty supper when you want something warming and substantial. Serve with a simple green side vegetable, such as the Italian-style Garlic Spinach (see page 31).

700 g/1½ lbs. braising beef, cubed

2 tablespoons olive oil

6 shallots, blanched and peeled

1 bay leaf

2–3 sprigs of fresh thyme

2 carrots, peeled and chopped

300 ml/1¼ cups brown ale

300 ml/1¼ cups beef or chicken stock

1 whole garlic clove, peeled

1 tablespoon freshly chopped parsley

salt and freshly ground black pepper

DUMPLINGS

125 g/1 cup self-raising/self-rising flour

75 g/¾ cup shredded suet

15 g/½ oz. wild garlic leaves/ramps, finely chopped

cold water, to mix

a lidded flameproof casserole dish

Serves 6

Preheat the oven to 180°C (350°F) Gas 4. Bring the beef to room temperature.

Heat 1½ tablespoons of the olive oil in a casserole dish until hot. Add the beef and fry, browning on all sides. Remove the beef and reserve.

Add the remaining olive oil to the casserole dish and heat through. Add the shallots and fry until lightly browned.

Return the browned beef to the casserole and add the bay leaf, thyme, carrots, brown ale, stock, garlic and parsley. Season with salt and pepper. Bring to the boil. Cover and cook in the preheated oven for 1½ hours until the beef is tender.

Towards the end of the cooking time, make the dumplings. In a bowl, mix together the flour, suet and wild garlic/ramps, seasoning well with salt and pepper. Add in cold water, 2–3 tablespoons at a time, and bring together to form a sticky dough. Shape into 6 even-sized round dumplings.

Add the dumplings to the casserole dish, allowing them to rest on the surface of the stew. Cover the casserole dish and return to the oven. Bake for a further 20 minutes until the dumplings have cooked and expanded. Serve at once.

Wild garlic/ramps miso pork stir-fry

Wild garlic/ramps has a great affinity with Asian flavourings, such as ginger, soy sauce and Japanese miso paste. Cooked in just minutes and served simply with rice or noodles, this pork dish makes a perfect midweek supper. If you wish, tofu could be used instead of pork.

1 tablespoon sunflower or vegetable oil

1 cm/½-in. fresh ginger, peeled and finely chopped

400 g/14 oz. lean pork fillet, sliced into 1-cm/½-in. strips

1 tablespoon rice wine or Amontillado sherry

1 tablespoon dark soy sauce

1 tablespoon dark miso paste

40 g/1½ oz. wild garlic leaves/ramps, rinsed well and chopped into 2.5-cm/1-in. lengths

Serves 4

Heat a wok until hot. Add the oil and heat through. Add the ginger and fry briefly, stirring, until fragrant.

Add the pork strips and fry, stirring, until lightened. Pour in the rice wine and allow to sizzle briefly. Add the soy sauce and miso paste and stir-fry for 2–3 minutes.

Add the wild garlic/ramps and stir-fry until just wilted. Check the pork has cooked through and serve at once.

For a vegetarian version of the dish, cube 400 g/14 oz. of firm tofu and pat dry. Add to the wok once the ginger is fragrant and stir-fry for 2–3 minutes until the tofu takes on a little colour. Proceed with the recipe as directed.

Wild garlic/ramps stoved new potatoes

This traditional, stovetop method of cooking potatoes results in a great combination of textures, with the crispy 'crust' and the soft, steamed potato. The potatoes take on a nutty sweetness flavoured by the wild garlic/ramps.

500 g/1 lb. 2 oz. new potatoes
2–3 tablespoons clarified butter, or 2 tablespoons olive oil mixed with 10 g/ 2 teaspoons butter
sea salt flakes, to season
25 g/1 oz. wild garlic leaves/ramps (or garlic chives if wild garlic is not in season), thoroughly rinsed and chopped into 2.5-cm/ 1-in. lengths

a heavy lidded frying pan/skillet

Serves 4

Chop the potatoes into even-sized chunks, roughly 3 x 2 cm/1¼ x ¾ inches.

Heat the clarified butter in the heavy, lidded frying pan/skillet until hot. Add in the potato pieces, flesh side down, arranging them in a single layer in the pan. Season with sea salt flakes and sprinkle over the chopped wild garlic/ramps.

Cover the pan and cook over a medium heat without disturbing the potatoes for 30 minutes until they are soft and tender. Carefully turn over the potatoes, revealing their crispy golden brown side and serve them this side up.

Wild garlic/ramps sweet potato mash

Wild garlic/ramps gives a savoury lift to mashed sweet potatoes. Serve with sausages or a chicken casserole for a tasty meal. As you peel the potatoes, place in water acidulated with a touch of vinegar or lemon juice to prevent discolouration.

900 g/2 lb. orange-fleshed sweet potatoes, peeled and chopped into even chunks
3½ tablespoons butter
50 g/2 oz. wild garlic leaves/ramps, thoroughly rinsed and finely chopped
splash of single/light cream
freshly grated nutmeg
salt and freshly ground black pepper

Serves 4

Boil the sweet potatoes in salted water until softened; drain well and return to the pan. Melt the butter in a small frying pan/skillet, add in the wild garlic/ramps and cook, stirring, until slightly wilted.

Add the wild garlic/ramps with the butter to the potatoes and a splash of cream. Mash together well. Season with freshly ground pepper and grated nutmeg. Serve at once.

Celebratory garlic

Garlic festivals

Garlic has always aroused strong emotions, with people either loving or loathing it. The conviction of those who love it is demonstrated by the number of festivals celebrating this pungent ingredient around the world, from Europe to North America.

Amongst the most famous of these is the Gilroy Garlic Festival, held each summer in the city of Gilroy in California, USA. It was well-respected Gilroy resident Dr Rudy Melone who, in 1978, came up with the idea of a festival celebrating the garlic harvest. He approached Don Christopher of the Christopher Ranch, a local grower and shipper of garlic, and

together the two of them co-founded the festival. Such has been the festival's success that it has become one of the largest food festivals in the US, attracting tens of thousands of visitors each year and raising large amounts of money for local charities. Run with both brio and professionalism by a committed team of volunteers, the event is a massive garlic-themed jamboree in the best American style. As one might expect, there is a plethora of garlic-flavoured foods on offer, including garlic gator, garlic burgers, garlic calamari, pesto and a signature garlic ice cream. Culinary garlic creativity is encouraged by the Great

Garlic Cook Off, which is open to amateur chefs across the US who must create original recipes using at least six cloves of garlic. Professional chefs are catered for with a garlic-themed Iron Chef-style showdown.

The Gilroy Garlic Festival has inspired festivals in other parts of the world, among them the Isle of Wight Garlic Festival, held on the British island since 1983. The community of Newchurch were looking for fundraising events to raise money for the local school. Farmer Colin Boswell, who had visited Gilroy, suggested the idea of a similar event and so the Isle of Wight Garlic Festival came into being. Offering a characterful combination of a 1960s-style pop festival and a country fair generously laced with all things garlic, the event attracts thousands of visitors and has become a fixture in the island's summer calendar.

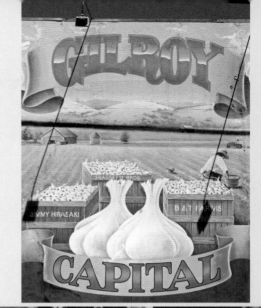

As one might expect, garlic festivals usually take place in areas where garlic is cultivated, offering the growers a chance to both celebrate and promote their crop and the work that goes into growing it. Voghiera, near Ferrara in Italy, has long been noted for its garlic, which has bright white large cloves and a delicate flavour, in 2007 it was granted a Protected Designation of Origin. Each summer the local authority holds the Fiera dell'Aglio di Voghiera DOP offering farmers the chance to sell their recently harvested garlic to the public and to talk about garlic's properties, while the garlic can be sampled in traditional dishes.

In Lautrec in France, late summer sees a festival celebrating the famed pink garlic of Lautrec. The garlic had traditionally been grown on a small scale but 1959 saw the founding of the splendidly named Defence Committee of the Pink Garlic of Lautrec, aimed at promoting and protecting this local speciality, with the garlic given Protected Geographical Indications status (PGI) in 1996. The Pink Garlic Festival, which has taken place since 1970, is held in August and features events such as a contest for the longest garlic plait and the chance to sample the local delicacy of garlic soup. It is a picturesque event to mark the harvest of a special local crop.

Crispy garlic chive chicken wontons

Deep-frying these dumplings until they are crisp transforms them into an appetizing snack – when served with the dipping sauce, they go perfectly with pre-dinner drinks. Chinese black rice vinegar is available from Asian stores.

1 chicken breast fillet (approx. 140 g/5 oz.), finely minced

4 tablespoons finely chopped fresh Chinese chives

a pinch of ground Sichuan pepper

1 teaspoon light soy sauce

½ teaspoon sesame oil

16 wonton wrappers

sunflower or vegetable oil, for deep frying

salt and freshly ground black pepper

DIPPING SAUCE

2 tablespoons Chinese black rice vinegar

1 teaspoon sugar

1 garlic clove, finely chopped

½ red chilli/chile, finely chopped (optional)

Serves 4

Thoroughly mix together the minced chicken, Chinese chives, Sichuan pepper, soy sauce and sesame oil. Season well with salt and pepper.

Mix together the ingredients for the dipping sauce and set aside.

Take a wonton wrapper and place a teaspoon of the chicken mixture in the centre of the wrapper. Brush the edges with a little cold water and bring the wrapper together over the chicken to form a parcel, pressing together well to seal properly. Set aside. Repeat the process until all 16 wrappers have been filled.

Heat the oil in a large saucepan until very hot. Add four of the wontons and fry for a few minutes, until golden brown on both sides, turning over halfway through to ensure even browning. Remove with a slotted spoon and drain on kitchen paper. Repeat the process with the remaining wontons.

Serve at once with the dipping sauce.

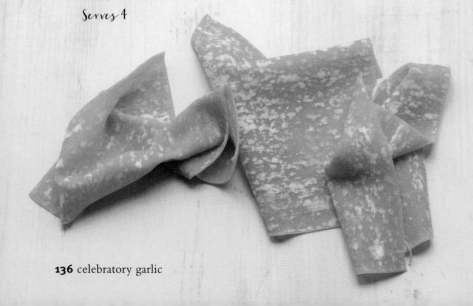

Steamed black garlic scallops

A luxurious seafood dish, with the natural sweetness of the scallops contrasting nicely with the savoury, smoky saltiness of the garlic dressing.

3 tablespoons dark soy sauce

2 black garlic cloves, finely chopped

2-cm/¾-in. fresh ginger, peeled and finely chopped

1 spring onion/scallion, finely chopped

12 king scallops

4 tablespoons groundnut or sunflower oil

2 black garlic cloves, finely chopped

a steamer

Serves 4 as an appetizer

Mix together the soy sauce, black garlic, ginger and spring onion/scallion in a bowl and set aside.

Steam the scallops until they turn opaque and are cooked through.

Heat the oil in a small frying pan/skillet, add the garlic and fry, stirring often, until fragrant. Pour the hot garlic oil into the soy sauce mixture, mixing well to form the dressing. Spoon the garlic dressing over the freshly steamed scallops and serve at once.

Risotto nero with garlic prawns/shrimp

A well-made risotto is always a treat. Black rice, cooked with squid ink and flavoured with fish stock, combined with pink prawns/shrimp makes a striking dish – one which tastes as good as it looks and is ideal for dinner parties.

1 litre/4 cups good-quality or homemade fish stock
3 tablespoons olive oil
1 shallot, finely chopped
3 garlic cloves, 2 finely chopped and 1 peeled but left whole
200-g/7-oz. squid, cleaned and chopped into small pieces
8-g/¼-fl .oz. sachet of squid ink
350 g/1 ¾ cups risotto rice
50 ml/3½ tablespoons dry white wine
25 g /1¾ tablespoons butter
12 raw tiger prawns/shrimp, heads removed, peeled and deveined
salt
chopped fresh parsley, to garnish

Serves 4

Bring the fish stock to a simmer in a large pan.

Heat 2 tablespoons of the olive oil in a separate, heavy-based saucepan. Add the shallot and chopped garlic and fry gently, stirring, until the shallot has softened. Add the squid and fry, continuing to stir, until whitened and opaque. Mix in the squid ink. Stir in the rice. Pour over the wine and cook, stirring, until reduced.

Add a ladleful of the simmering stock to the rice and cook, stirring, until absorbed. Repeat the process until all the stock has been added and the rice is cooked through. Taste and season with salt as needed. Stir in the butter and set aside to rest briefly.

Heat the remaining oil in a frying pan/skillet. Once frothing, add the whole garlic clove and fry, stirring, until fragrant. Add the prawns/shrimp with a pinch of salt and fry, stirring, until the prawns/shrimp have turned pink and opaque and are cooked through. Discard the garlic clove.

Serve each portion of the risotto rice topped with prawns/shrimp and garnished with parsley.

Griddled tuna with garlic bean purée and gremolata

Gremolata – traditionally served with osso buco – also goes very well with fish. Here firm-textured tuna steaks contrast nicely with the soft bean purée, while gremolata adds a refreshing zip. A great dish to make for dinner parties.

2 x 400-g/14-oz. cans
  of butter beans/lima beans
  in water
2 tablespoons olive oil
1 onion, finely chopped
1 garlic clove, finely chopped
4 tuna steaks, each
  approx. 200 g/7 oz.
salt and freshly ground black
  pepper
extra virgin olive oil, to garnish

GREMOLATA
2 garlic cloves
pinch of salt
finely grated zest of 2 lemons
6 tablespoons finely chopped
  fresh parsley

a griddle pan

Serves 4

First, make the gremolata. Crush the garlic cloves with a pinch of salt to a paste. Mix together with the lemon zest and parsley and set aside.

Drain the beans, reserving 4 tablespoons of the bean water. Heat 1 tablespoon of the olive oil in a heavy saucepan. Add the onion and garlic and fry gently, stirring, until softened. Add the drained butter beans and reserved bean water, mixing in. Cover and cook gently for 10 minutes, stirring now and then. Mash into a purée, season with salt and pepper and keep warm until serving.

Preheat the griddle pan until very hot. Coat the tuna steaks with the remaining olive oil and season with salt and pepper. Griddle the tuna steaks until cooked to taste (about 2–3 minutes per side), turning occasionally to ensure even cooking.

Spoon the gremolata over the griddled tuna steaks and serve on a bed of bean purée, spooning over a little extra virgin olive oil for flavour and moisture.

2 tablespoons olive oil

2 shallots, finely chopped

1 celery stalk, finely chopped

2 garlic cloves, chopped

2 bay leaves

5 sprigs of thyme

½ teaspoon fennel seeds

50 ml/3½ tablespoons Pernod or dry white wine

400-g/14-oz. can of chopped tomatoes

50 ml/3½ tablespoons freshly squeezed orange juice

1 teaspoon grated orange zest

a pinch of saffron strands, finely ground and soaked in 1 tablespoon hot water

a pinch of Turkish chilli/ Aleppo hot pepper flakes

500 ml/2 cups fish stock

a handful of freshly chopped parsley, plus extra to garnish

500 g/1 lb. 2 oz. fish fillet, skinned and chopped into chunks

200 g/7 oz. raw prawns/ shrimp, peeled and heads removed, deveined

150 g/5½ oz. squid rings

salt and freshly ground black pepper

chopped fresh parsley, to garnish

a deep sauté pan

Serves 4

Mediterranean garlicky fish stew

An appealingly colourful dish, perfect for a hot summer's day and ideal for entertaining. Serve with slices of baguette to soak up the fragrant broth.

Heat the olive oil in the deep sauté pan. Add the shallots and fry gently, stirring often, until softened and lightly browned. Add the celery, garlic, bay leaves, thyme and fennel seeds and fry, stirring, for 2 minutes until fragrant.

Pour in the Pernod or white wine and fry, stirring, until largely reduced. Mix in the chopped tomatoes and cook, stirring often, until thickened and reduced. Stir in the orange juice and zest, saffron soaking water and chilli/hot pepper flakes. Add the fish stock. Taste and season with salt and pepper accordingly. Mix in the parsley.

Bring to the boil and cook for 5 minutes. Add in the fish, prawns and squid rings and simmer until just cooked through – this takes just a matter of minutes. Garnish with parsley and serve at once.

Braised garlic pork bao

Smooth-textured, pillowy Taiwanese-style buns contrast beautifully with the gutsy, succulent braised pork, making this a memorably tasty treat.

BRAISED PORK

1 tablespoon oil

1 onion, finely chopped

2 garlic cloves, chopped

2-cm/¾-in. fresh ginger, peeled and chopped

400 g/14 oz. pork belly, cut into 2.5-cm/1-in. cubes

1 tablespoon Korean soy bean paste

1 tablespoon Korean chilli paste

1 tablespoon dark soy sauce

1 tablespoon rice wine or medium sherry

1 teaspoon sugar

300 ml/1¼ cups chicken stock or water

BAO (TAIWANESE BUNS)

250 g/1¾ cups plain/ all-purpose flour

2 teaspoons caster/ granulated sugar

½ teaspoon fast-action dried yeast

½ teaspoon baking powder

¼ teaspoon salt

100 ml/⅓ cup hand-hot water

50 ml/3½ tablespoons whole milk

2 teaspoons white wine vinegar

shredded carrot and spring onion/scallion, to garnish

a large lidded frying pan/skillet or casserole dish

a steamer

Makes 8

First make the braised pork. Heat the oil in a large lidded frying pan/skillet or casserole dish. Fry the onion, garlic and ginger for 2 minutes, stirring, until the onion has softened and the mixture is fragrant. Add the chopped pork belly and fry, stirring often, until the pork is lightly browned.

Add the soy bean and chilli pastes and mix to coat thoroughly. Add the soy sauce, rice wine and sugar and cook, stirring, for 1 minute. Add the stock or water and bring to the boil.

Cover with a lid, reduce the heat and simmer for 1 hour until the pork is tender. Uncover the pan, increase the heat to bring the liquid to the boil and cook uncovered over medium heat, stirring often, until the sauce has considerably reduced. Set aside.

To make the bao, mix together the flour, sugar, yeast, baking powder and salt in a large bowl. Add in the hand-hot water, milk and vinegar and mix together to form a soft dough. Knead for 10 minutes until the dough is supple and smooth.

Place the dough in an oiled bowl, cover with oiled cling film/plastic wrap and set aside in a warm place for an hour to rise.

On a lightly floured surface, knock back the risen dough and roll to form a thick sausage shape. Cut into 8 even-sized pieces and shape each piece into a ball.

Roll each dough ball into an oval, roughly 12-cm/5-in. long. Fold each oval in half over a small rectangular piece of parchment paper. Cover with oiled clingfilm/plastic wrap and set aside to rest for 20 minutes.

Line the steamer with oiled parchment paper. Steam the buns in batches, spaced apart, for 10 minutes or until cooked through.

Handling the hot buns carefully, remove the parchment paper. Fill each bun with braised pork, garnish with shredded carrot and spring onion/scallion and serve at once.

Rosemary, garlic and fennel roast pork

Fragrant rosemary, aromatic fennel and tasty garlic combine to good effect with this simple but flavourful roast pork dish.

1.8-kg/4-lb. pork loin, skin scored for crackling, chined*

1 tablespoon fennel seeds

1 teaspoon olive oil

2 garlic cloves, peeled and cut into slivers

3–4 rosemary sprigs, chopped into short pieces

salt and freshly ground black pepper

*Note: the chine is a tough cut of meat which is usually removed in supermarket meat but may need to be trimmed if bought from the butcher, or you can ask your butcher to do this for you.

Serves 4–6

Preheat the oven to 220°C (425°F) Gas 7. Bring the pork to room temperature.

Dry-fry the fennel seeds until fragrant, then cool and finely grind.

Pat the pork dry with paper towels. Season with salt and plenty of pepper, rubbing the salt into the skin.

Rub the pork with the ground fennel, then cut small incisions in the flesh. Rub the flesh with olive oil, then insert the garlic slivers and rosemary into the incisions. Place the pork in a roasting pan.

Roast the pork for 15 minutes in the preheated oven, then reduce the oven temperature to 180°C (350°F) Gas 4 and roast for a further 1½ hours until cooked through. Set aside to rest in a warm place for 20 minutes before carving. Serve with the roasting juices.

Garlicky chicken livers with pomegranate molasses

A classic from Lebanon, this simple but tasty dish of soft, tender chicken livers is given a pleasant sour tang by the pomegranate molasses and lemon juice. Serve as an appetizer or as part of a mezze meal.

3 tablespoons olive oil
1 garlic clove, sliced lengthways
400 g/14 oz. chicken livers
1 tablespoon pomegranate molasses
freshly squeezed juice juice of ½ lemon
1 tablespoon pomegranate kernels (optional)
salt and freshly ground black pepper
chopped fresh parsley, to garnish
bread, to serve

Serves 4

Heat the olive oil in a large, heavy frying pan/skillet. Add the sliced garlic and fry briefly, stirring, until fragrant. Add the chicken livers and fry, stirring frequently, for 3–5 minutes. Don't overcook the livers, as this would make them tough to eat. Season with salt and pepper.

Add the pomegranate molasses and lemon juice to the frying pan/skillet. Cook briefly, stirring to coat the livers in the liquid.

Serve at once, garnished with pomegranate kernels, if using, and parsley with bread on the side to soak up the juices.

Fragrant garlic lamb shanks with apricots

Slow-cooking is ideal for lamb shanks. This recipe delivers great results with tender, aromatic spiced meat. Serve this flavourful, fragrant lamb dish with couscous or rice.

2 tablespoons olive oil
4 even-sized lamb shanks
2 onions, finely chopped
2 garlic cloves, chopped
1 celery stalk, finely chopped
1 carrot, peeled and finely sliced
1 cinnamon stick
1 teaspoon ground ginger
½ teaspoon ground cinnamon
a pinch of saffron strands, ground and soaked in 1 tablespoon warm water
½ teaspoon freshly ground black pepper
3 tablespoons tomato purée/paste
salt
12 dried, unsulphured apricots
1 tablespoon clear honey
½ teaspoon rose water, optional
3 tablespoons flaked/ slivered almonds, dry-fried until golden
chopped fresh coriander/ cilantro, to garnish

a large lidded casserole dish

Serves 4

Preheat the oven to 150°C (300°F) Gas 2.

Heat 1 tablespoon of the olive oil in a large frying pan/skillet. Add the lamb shanks and fry until browned on all sides. Remove from the heat.

Heat the remaining olive oil in the large casserole dish. Add the onions, garlic, celery, carrot and cinnamon stick and fry gently, stirring, until the onion has softened and the mixture is fragrant. Mix in the ginger, ground cinnamon, saffron water and black pepper, then the tomato purée/paste. Add the browned lamb shanks and mix to coat well.

Pour in enough water to just cover the lamb. Season with salt. Bring to the boil. Cover and transfer to the preheated oven to cook for 2 hours, adding the dried apricots after 1½ hours of cooking time.

When the lamb is tender and cooked, stir in the honey and rose water, garnish with flaked almonds and chopped coriander/cilantro and serve at once.

Garlic anchovy roast lamb

Adding a few classic flavourings to lamb before roasting it is a simple step that transforms the finished dish. As the lamb cooks, the anchovy fillets 'melt' into the dish, adding an extra umami touch to the tender lamb. Serve with new potatoes and broccoli, green beans or brussel tops.

1 leg of lamb, approx.
  1.5 kg/3¼ lbs.
2 garlic cloves, chopped into
  slivers
5 anchovy fillets, chopped
  into short pieces
3 fresh rosemary sprigs, cut
  into short pieces
40 g/3 tablespoons butter,
  softened
150 ml/⅔ cup red wine
salt and freshly ground black
  pepper

GRAVY
300 ml/1¼ cups chicken
  stock or water

Serves 4–6

Preheat the oven to 230°C (450°F) Gas 8. Bring the lamb to room temperature.

Season the lamb with salt and pepper. Using a small, sharp knife, cut little incisions in the lamb flesh on all sides of the leg. Take a piece each of garlic, anchovy and rosemary and insert the flavourings into an incision, making sure to push the garlic into the flesh. Repeat the process until the garlic has been used up.

Mash any remaining anchovy and rosemary leaves into the softened butter. Place the lamb in a roasting tray and smear the butter over the fleshy part of the lamb. Pour over the red wine.

Roast the lamb in the preheated oven for 15 minutes. Reduce the oven temperature to 180°C (350°F) Gas 4 and roast for a further 45 minutes for medium rare or 30–35 minutes for rare, basting now and then with the wine roasting juices.

Remove from the oven and rest in a warm place for 30 minutes.

To make the gravy, de-glaze the roasting pan – place it on the stovetop, add the stock or water and bring to the boil. Scrape the pan with a wooden spoon to release the flavoursome brown residues so they combine with the liquid.

Serve the lamb with the roasting juice gravy on the side.

Index

Picture credits

All photography by Clare Winfield apart from pages:

12 Lynn Keddie/Getty Images
13al karandaev/Getty Images
13ar HandmadePictures/Getty Images
13br Gus Filgate
34 Kent Chan/EyeEm/Getty Images
35 Dario Sartini/Getty Images
64l Tim Graham/Getty Images
64r ManuelVelasco/istock
65 Lucinda Symons
86 rdparis22/Getty Images
87 eag1e/Getty Images

95 Ian Wallace
110l-11l David Merewether and Caroline Hughes
111r Erin Kunkel
134 Jeremy Woodhouse/Getty Images
135a Danita Delimont/Getty Images
135b Krzysztof Dydynski/Getty Images

Key: a = above; b = below;
r = right; l = left;

Acknowledgments

My loving thanks to my family and friends who gave me feedback and support as I tested the garlic recipes for the book.

Many thanks for their help in sourcing ingredients to Nicola Lando of the brilliant Souschef, the wonderfully helpful John and Elena at Spa Terminus and Parkway Greens. Thank you, too, to committed garlic growers Mark Botwright of Southwest Garlic Farm, the Gamots of La Maison de l'Ail and Alley Swiss of Filaree Garlic Farm.

A book is a team effort and working with Ryland, Peters and Small is always a pleasure. Thank you, Cindy Richards and Julia Charles for commissioning this book on an ingredient I love and to Gillian Haslam and Alice Sambrook for your work editing it. It's a beautiful book – thank you, Clare Winfield for your delicious food photography, Rachel Wood for food styling, Jo Harris for prop styling and Sonya Nathoo for her art direction and design.